P9-EDA-341

DOING TIME ON THE OUTSIDE:
DECONSTRUCTING THE BENEVOLENT COMMUNITY

Criminalized women are a subject of growing interest in contemporary sociological research. However, much of the work in this area has focused on imprisonment, and little attention has been paid to women serving their sentences in the community. *Doing Time on the Outside* fills a gap in the research by studying the experiences of women on conditional release, and attempting to explain how some criminalized women avoid going back into custody given the many challenges they face.

Using information collected in a series of interviews, MaDonna R. Maidment identifies four major findings related to criminalized women's reintegration into the community. First, the fewer layers of social control a woman lived under prior to her prison term, the greater her chances of staying out of prison. Those women accustomed to a lifetime of formal social controls are vulnerable and largely dependent on continued intervention. Second, women's own accounts of their success do not coincide with official definitions. For many women who have spent their lives being controlled by state agencies, sustaining a relatively short period of independence in the community is a major milestone. Third, for those women who have managed to stay out of the criminal justice system, a majority remain tightly entangled in other state-sponsored control regimes, where patterns of dependency, medicalization, and infantilization still persist in the treatment of women. Fourth, familial and social support networks are paramount to women's successful reintegration, far more than professional supports provided by state and community agencies.

Maidment's conclusions have important political and social implications: they urge us to re-examine how correctional systems treat criminalized women, and to call into question current policies that fail to take into account the economic, social, and cultural realities of women's lives.

MADONNA R. MAIDMENT is an assistant professor in the Department of Sociology and Anthropology at the University of Guelph.

OKANAGAN COLLEGE
LIBRARY
BRITISH COLUMBIA

MADONNA R. MAIDMENT

Doing Time on the Outside

Deconstructing the Benevolent Community

UNIVERSITY OF TORONTO PRESS
Toronto Buffalo London

© University of Toronto Press Incorporated 2006
Toronto Buffalo London
Printed in Canada

ISBN-13: 978-0-8020-9080-5 (cloth)
ISBN-10: 0-8020-9080-X (cloth)
ISBN-13: 978-0-8020-9389-9 (paper)
ISBN-10: 0-8020-9389-2 (paper)

Printed on acid-free paper

Library and Archives Canada Cataloguing in Publication

Maidment, MaDonna R. (MaDonna Rose)
Doing time on the outside : deconstructing the benevolent community /
Madonna R. Maidment.

Includes bibliographical references and index.
ISBN-13: 978-0-8020-9080-5 (bound)
ISBN-10: 0-8020-9080-X (bound)
ISBN-13: 978-0-8020-9389-9 (pbk.)
ISBN-10: 0-8020-9389-2 (pbk.)

1. Women prisoners – Canada – Social conditions. 2. Female offenders –
Canada – Social conditions. 3. Women – Social conditions. I. Title.

HV6046.M34 2006   365'.60820971   C2006-903332-3

This book has been published with the help of a grant from the Canadian
Federation for the Humanities and Social Sciences, through the Aid to
Scholarly Publications Programme, using funds provided by the Social
Sciences and Humanities Research Council of Canada.

University of Toronto Press acknowledges the financial assistance to its
publishing program of the Canada Council for the Arts and the Ontario
Arts Council.

University of Toronto Press acknowledges the financial support for its
publishing activities of the Government of Canada through the Book
Publishing Industry Development Program (BPIDP).

Contents

Acknowledgements   vii

Introduction   3

1 Penal Controls on Criminalized Women   14

2 Sociopolitical Context of Criminalizing Women   33

3 Stumbling Blocks to 'Corrections' Research   47

4 Getting In: Pathways to Prison   57

5 Doing Time on the Inside: Prisoning of Women   82

6 Getting Out: Immediate and Measurable Transitions   102

7 State and Localized Controls   123

Conclusion: Where to from Here?   146

Appendix: Research Guide   153

Notes   157

References   165

Index   179

Acknowledgments

This book is marked by the passing of my beloved father, Eldon (Coute) Maidment, whom I love and miss unquantifiably. The title of this work, *Doing Time on the Outside*, is borrowed from his repertoire of insightful observations on social injustice. His resonant wisdom would fill volumes. I continue to flourish from the wisdom, unwavering guidance, and organic intellect of my mother, Dianne Flynn, who is my salient mentor and humanitarian role model. I am truly blessed to have the support of my sisters Cathy, Lisa, and Carole, brother Gerry, and stepfather Brian. The fruits of our lengthy and challenging discussions on issues of social injustice over many years are reflected in this work.

I am very fortunate to have forged a friendship with a number of women involved in the struggle for social change. These wonderful women share a vision and commitment to equality and continue to blaze trails in advancing social justice. Dorothy Proctor, Kim Pate, Joyce Hancock, Rebecca Woodrow, Kathy Kendall, and Kelly Hannah-Moffat have collectively influenced my work in distinguishable ways over the years. It is in their engaged spirit of activism and academia that I strive towards a critical appraisal of people at the margins. I am most indebted, as always, to the extraordinarily courageous and spirited women who agreed to take part in this research, to share their stories and their lives, and open their homes and hearts to me. You are the true scholars.

Throughout my academic career, I have been extremely privileged to enjoy the company and intellectual rigour of a number of critical sociologists. Walter DeKeseredy (University of Ontario Institute of Technology), Colette Parent (University of Ottawa), Wallace Clement (Carleton University), Susan Caringella-McDonald (Western Michigan University), and Andreas Tomaszewski (Eastern Michigan University) have each influenced my thinking in distinguishable ways. I thank you ever so much for your collective contributions to strengthening my work.

This research has been supported financially through a number of sources including the Social Sciences and Humanities Research Council (SSHRC), Carleton University Faculty of Graduate Studies and Research, and the Ontario Ministry of Education (Ontario Graduate Scholarship). Finally, but in no small way, the faculty and staff in the Sociology department at Memorial University have always been a major source of support and inspiration for my work over many years. In particular, I acknowledge the collegiality of Dr Larry Felt for sharing his data set on criminalized women. To my colleagues in the department of Sociology and Anthropology at the University of Guelph, a sincere expression of gratitude for taking a chance on me so early on in my academic career, thereby facilitating my efforts to complete this book.

DOING TIME ON THE OUTSIDE:
DECONSTRUCTING THE BENEVOLENT COMMUNITY

Introduction

The experience of imprisonment is not one to equip a woman to cope more effectively with life.

Eaton (1993: 174)

The 1990s were ushered in on the promise of 'correctional'[1] renewal for criminalized women in Canada. Sociopolitical pressure in the years prior to the launch of a 'reformist agenda' came to bear on the federal government to overhaul its ideological approach to criminalized women. Subsequent inquiries and government reports (most notably the Task Force on Federally Sentenced Women 1990; and the Arbour Commission Report 1996) highlighted the deficiencies of women's prisons and called for a woman-centred[2] approach to guide both substantive and ideological reforms. However, any illusion of change has been deflated over the years with mounting evidence that not only does the criminal (in)justice system not reform, it continues to violate the basic human rights of prisoners (Canadian Human Rights Commission 2003). Despite propaganda by the federal government of a progressive penal strategy for women, corrections remains a repressive tool of the state used to responsibilize (Kemshall 2002) and pathologize (Pollack and Kendall 2005) women both inside and outside the prison.

The well-documented shortcomings of women-centred corrections (see Pollack and Kendall 2005; Neve and Pate 2005; Horii 2000; Hannah-Moffat and Shaw 2000) and the purported emphasis on empowerment[3] (Hannah-Moffat 2000; Pollack 2000) have focused almost exclusively on federally *incarcerated*[4] women in Canada. Critical inquiry has eclipsed the overlay of any such reform at the local level. To date, there has been a peculiar absence of assessing how a woman-centred approach and its attendant principles would apply outside the prison. This book seeks to narrow this persisting gap. In doing so, I move beyond an examination of well-established, albeit crucial factors, that propel women back into prison (such as inadequate housing, lack of meaningful employment and training, and lack of family supports) and focus on the control trajectories of criminalized women; the structural and systemic inequalities that contribute to criminalizing women; and the omnipresent control functions of penology at the local level. Moreover, this book critically assesses the incongruency between artificial principles of penal policy (that is, the overpronounced risk and/or need markers enshrined in penology) and the socioeconomic inequalities of women's lives. Women who manage to complete their conditional releases are not suddenly becoming gainfully employed, securing safe and affordable housing, reuniting with children and families, developing strong peer supports, and developing 'pro-social' attitudes, all of which have been well-established as success predictors in the penal lexicon of risk management. Rather, something more, or something quite different, is happening in women's lives after incarceration. That is, wherein the criminal (in)justice system releases its control of women, other state-run and localized[5] agencies are stepping in to replace formal control. Therefore, while women probationers and/or parolees may avoid a return to prison, they seldom break free of the legal (Comack and Balfour 2004), medical (Conrad and Schneider 1985), and 'psy'-entific professions (psychology, psychiatry, and psychopharmacology; see Kendall and Pollack 2005; Ingleby 1983) that operate locally to regulate women's lives long after the expiration of their prison sentences.

Entrenched dependencies and transcarceral controls are a prominent feature of localized penal sanctions. The conceptual underpinnings of transcarceration build upon the work of Michel Foucault (1977) and his argument that 'discipline and surveillance create a more extensive form of power ... in which the power to punish is inserted more deeply and more certainly into the social fabric. The advent of non-segregative techniques of control has resulted in more control, not less, as the control net is widened and its mesh thinned' (cited in Lowman, Menzies, and Palys 1987: 9). Although transcarceration and transinstitutionalization are often used interchangeably, 'it is not simply in institutional terms that the impact of changing control strategies must be conceptualized ... transinstitutionalization ... can only offer a partial understanding of the modern education-health-welfare-criminal-justice complex. It confines the understanding of control strategies to their institutional expression' (ibid.). Transcarceration captures the 'holistic and diffused character of state power over dependents and deviants, and its permeation through the regulatory systems of civil society' (ibid.: 2). Suffice it to say that women's entanglement with/in the criminal justice system *and* with other state and/or local agencies continues to prioritize self-regulation through formal control measures.

For both pragmatic and theoretical reasons, insight into the lives of criminalized women after time spent in prison is needed. Canada, like other industrialized nations, has become increasingly reliant on conditional release programs wherein the majority of criminalized men and women are now under some form of localized control. In July 2003, of the 822 women serving federal sentences in Canada, 374 (45%) were institutionalized while 448 (55%) were under some form of conditional release. By contrast, 61 per cent (12,221 out of 20,029) of federally sentenced men were incarcerated while 39 per cent were conditionally released (Canadian Human Rights Commission 2003). Moreover, the success[6] rates of women who complete their conditional sentences are quite high. The official recidivism rate for federally sentenced women is roughly 22 per cent, compared with 59 per cent for men. Furthermore, only 1 to 2 per cent of women returning to prison have committed a new crime while the majority are reapprehended for technical or administrative breaches of their often untenable parole conditions. Given the high numbers of women who complete their conditional release, it is far more fruitful to refocus attention to those who stay out of prison rather than narrowing our gaze to those who go back.

This book begins from the implicit assumption that a huge potential exists to learn more about 'what works' in 'corrections' by focusing on the majority of women who stay out of prison. In doing so, four intersectional patterns chronicling women's lives post-prison are brought into view. The foremost finding is that the chances of staying out of prison increase dramatically for women who have managed to escape a formalized history of state control (namely, child custody interventions, welfare caseworkers, and mental health agents) prior to entering prison.

Second, strict categorical definitions of *success* do not coincide with official definitions. Recidivism rates are inaccurate measures of quantifying women's successes and/or failures post-release. For many women whose entire lives have been controlled by state agencies, managing a relatively short period of quasi-independence upon release constitutes a major victory. Therefore, beginning from the measurement of success based on recidivism rates undermines women's own accounts of their successes.

Third, among women who do manage to stay out of prison, a majority remain tightly entangled in other state-sponsored control networks. Patterns of dependency, medicalization, and infantilization persist in the treatment of women at a local level. Transcarceration, primarily under the guise of criminal justice and mental health agencies, pervades the lives of women who have spent most of their youth and adulthood under formalized controls. Moreover, state controls are often disguised as underfunded and under-resourced community groups that are forced to operate at the behest of state agendas.

Fourth, interpersonal relationships and social support networks are of paramount importance to women's successful 'reintegration.'[7] For women who maintain supportive kinship ties during their incarceration and subsequent release, the chances of staying out of prison are increased dramatically over those for women who do not enjoy such positive interpersonal relationships. Varying levels of professional interventions (such as probation and/or parole officers, psychiatrists and psychological counsellors, and residential case workers) play a less transformative role in determining women's successful reintegration. In fact, continued surveillance by localized agents is met by women with the same resistance as that which plays out in the prison reacting to the imbalanced power relations between the 'keepers' and the 'kept.'

Locating the Research

By now, the reader has no doubt sensed my need for problematizing penal language. Before proceeding further, I need to offload the tensions inherent in doing 'corrections' research. Researching and writing this book has given me a considerable (and ongoing) degree of frustration for two main reasons: First, because the criminal justice system is artificially set up to be separate from other social institutions, attention is deflected from other structures of oppression. Increasingly, under a neoliberal regime of governance, the 'criminalized' are depicted through media accounts and penal ideologies as disconnected from wider sociopolitical arenas. Criminality is held to be an individual problem and portrayed as the fault of the 'antisocial,' 'cognitively deficient' person who is unable to cope or 'think right' in society. Second, the language of penology is exclusionary and euphemistic. (I will speak more on resisting language in a later section.) The language and concomitant ideologies of penology are so well-entrenched that it becomes an ongoing struggle to deconstruct its superficially benign meanings at every turn. Suffice it to say that even upon completion of this book, I still struggle with breaking out of the 'correctional straitjacket' that is imposed by language and its inherent assumptions about criminalized populations. I share this tension early on so that the reader is able to interpret the rationale for paying close attention to the problematics of penal discourse.

I also share this conundrum so the reader is able to follow the methodological design and implementation of this study (detailed in chapter 3). When I began my research for this book I did fall prey (despite what I considered at the time to be an awareness of many of these inherent problems) to much of the conventional language and attendant practices that perpetuate the notion that there is something distinguishable and treatable between criminalized and non-criminalized populations (more on this false dichotomy later). Moreover, I accepted in many ways the popular notion that this research would uncover discernible differences between those women who make it out of prison and those women who remain entangled in the criminal justice system throughout their adult lives. At the outset, then, the overarching question driving my research was framed in the following way: How is it that some criminalized women, following further marginalization and institutionalization brought about by their prison experiences manage to avoid going back into custody while others do not? However, the more I moved forward the more I found fault with this line of inquiry. Adopting this framework traps one into accepting language and ideology that assume a treatable subject such that if we could but uncover the secret to 'success,' which according to neoliberal rhetoric lies with the individual, we could put an end to, or at least minimize, that individual's cycle of criminality. The lives of the women profiled in this book are much more complex than this 'risk management' formula would suggest. These women's lives are characterized by societal failings at every turn and cannot be viewed through the myopic lens of criminal justice to the exclusion of other social institutions.

As the research moved further along at the pre-testing phase, I still struggled with reconciling the inadequacy of penal discourse with the complexity of women's lives. In doing so, I necessarily expanded the scope of inquiry to include questions aimed at uncovering how *success* is defined? and by whom? What are the factors that contribute to women's criminalization in the first place? How does the 'prisoning'[8] of women contribute to success or failure? And how does the interplay with other social institutions affect women on conditional release? Even with this broadening of scope at the pre-testing stage, these guiding departures of inquiry underwent a further transformation and repositioning throughout the analyses of the data. It becomes increasingly more evident that women's attempts to negotiate their lives post-incarceration have very little to do with officially sanctioned characteristics – dynamic and legal indicators[9] – and much more to do with state-sponsored strategies of control that operate both within and apart from the criminal (in)justice system and alongside persistent socioeconomic inequalities in other systems to account for the ever-increasing overlapping of regulations in women's lives.

While situating these tensions upfront, I did move to designing a study that employed both quantitative and qualitative methodologies to provide insight into the plight of criminalized women in an eastern Canadian province. The sociodemographic profile of all sentenced women in the province of Newfoundland and Labrador (n = 359) over an eleven-year period (1990 to 2000) served as the starting point for analysing penal trends. Semistructured interviews were then carried out with twenty-two prisoners and ex-prisoners. Interviews were constructed to compare the experiences of two groups: (1) repeatedly criminalized women,[10] defined as those having more than four prison admissions, who returned to prison within a two-year period of their release; and (2) repeatedly criminalized women who managed to avoid a return to prison past the requisite two-year period.[11] By chronicling the systemic barriers that exist in society (such as the feminization of poverty, women's child care responsibilities, lack of familial and peer supports, and the medicalization of criminalized women) and the structural barriers within prisons (such as gender-blind standardized risk assessments, mandatory 'treatment,' lack of gender-based programming, and lack of services for mental health detainees) the strategies that women employ to stay out of prison are drawn out.

Locating the Researcher

Feminist epistemologies have contributed to the now common and useful practice whereby researchers locate themselves in a direct position to their research to demonstrate the subjective and biased nature of social scientific research. This not only enables the reader to examine the interconnectedness between the research topic and the researcher's social location but, more importantly, it is a worthwhile exercise for researchers to grapple with the preconceived notions that they themselves have about the study and its subsequent results. In understanding the relationship between researcher and researched (whereby traditionally only the biographies of the researched are revealed) this practice is important to shed light also on the relevant biography of the researcher. Since researchers are active participants in the data collection process, it is imperative that their positions be known and understood regarding factors like gender, race and/or ethnicity, and class before interpreting the data. Hertz emphasizes a framework for positioning the researcher, noting that 'through personal accounting, researchers must become more aware of how their own positions and interests are imposed at all stages of the research process – from the questions they ask to those they ignore, from who they study to who they ignore, from problem formulation to analysis, representation, and writing – in order to produce less distorted accounts of the social world' (1997: viii).

Feminist researchers attempting to garner a fuller understanding of women's experiences are also enabled through the closely connected process of reflexivity, achieved by 'reflecting upon and understanding our own personal, political, and intellectual autobiographies as researchers and making explicit where we are located in relation to our research respondents. Reflexivity also means acknowledging the critical role we play in creating, interpreting, and theorizing research data. Reflexivity during the data collection process requires constant and intensive scrutiny of what we know and how we come to know as researchers. This involves a process of actively constructing interpretations of field experiences and then interpreting how those experiences came about' (Mauthner and Doucet 1998: 121).

Starting from epistemological bases, my personal journey towards undertaking this study derives from my experiences as a working-class, heterosexual, white, urban woman in a relatively small Canadian Census Metropolitan Area (CMA). I have long recognized the fine line that I have traversed between the official status of 'offender' and 'non-offender.'[12] The question driving this current research could easily be expanded to reflect my long-standing attempts to understand how it is that some girls and women from lower working-class, disenfranchised backgrounds avoid the criminalizing process in the first place (or avoid getting caught and subsequently labelled[13]) while others do not. This begins as the overarching query imposing on my research as I take inventory of classmates, neighbours, and friends who have ended up on the 'other side of the law' while I managed to escape that fate. This is another project for another time but one that is constantly in the front of my mind as I meet and conduct research with 'women in trouble,' many of whom once sat in an elementary-school classroom alongside me.

My personal connection to this research morphed into a political grounding for change with the realization that in order to effect social change I needed to position myself to influence macro-social policy development. The conversion of 'private troubles' into 'public issues,' as formulated by C. Wright Mills (1959) was the driving force behind my thinking. The political momentum developed early in my undergraduate career as I began challenging the decision-making that unevenly discriminated among and against members of our society based primarily on divisions of class, race, gender, and sexuality. When nearing the completion of my liberal arts degree, I conducted a study of women who were sentenced to electronic house arrest and was alarmed at the incongruency of women's dual status as prisoners and full-time caregivers in their own homes. Evidently the gender-blind criminal justice system failed to acknowledge women's roles as primary caregivers and their concomitant responsibilities for domestic tasks both within and outside the home. The criminal justice system confines women within the domestic sphere while at the same time making absolutely no allowance for societal expectations of their roles as mothers, thereby setting them up for failure in one or both systems.

Later on, graduate research endorsed the notion of penology as an androcentric enterprise and the *community* as a 'catch-all' that escapes the critical interrogation afforded the prison. The extant penal literature neglects almost entirely the realities facing women (and men) upon their return to the very places where their troubles began. The whole notion of *reintegration* became a major area of inquiry as I watched women return (integrate) to the very same socially and economically disadvantaged locations that had brought them into 'conflict with the law' in the first place. The concept of reintegration, then, is an ambiguous one based on white, male, middle-class values, norms, and expectations.

Around this same time, I got involved with the Canadian Association of Elizabeth Fry Societies (CAEFS)[14] and co-founded the local branch of Elizabeth Fry in Newfoundland and Labrador. Increasingly, I was being sensitized to the neglect of criminalized women internationally, nationally, and locally. All the while, I was witnessing the realities facing women upon return to their neighbourhoods and the growing number of social, cultural, political, and economic forces competing to bring women down and keep them down including poverty, inadequate child care services, lack of education, lack of employment opportunities, histories of sexual and physical abuse, and the criminalization of mental illness. The concept of reintegration against the backdrop of these broader systemic barriers facing women in their communities seemed (oxy)moronic.

My research comes full circle back to the question of why some women become entangled in the criminal justice system in the first place. More precisely, the inquiry moves towards an understanding of the converging factors that contribute not only to women's initial criminalization but also to their continued, almost daily struggle to stay 'out of trouble.' Suffice it to say that I come at this research with a number of perplexing questions that have not been satisfactorily addressed in the criminological literature. For many social scientists, areas of overarching personal standpoint inform and drive our research agendas, and this is very much the impetus for my work.

Organization of the Book

Chapter 1 addresses the inherent problematics in doing *corrections* research. Interrogating the discourse used to set women in opposition to the social, economic, political, and cultural constructs of society that then contribute to their violating gender and legal norms is tackled. Feminist theories (socialist and standpoint) and epistemologies are discussed to locate the patriarchal and capitalist underpinnings of criminalizing women. I pay close attention to the subjectivities of knowledge construction and/or legitimation based on classist, racist and sexist world-views.

Chapter 2 continues the important work of locating criminalized women within a broader sociopolitical framework. Structural and systemic factors contributing to women's criminal pathways are examined. Ideological debates surrounding the discourse of women's penality are investigated against the backdrop of neoliberal and neo-conservative agendas that influence penal decision-making. From here, the international reputation of Canada as the benevolent jailer is unravelled.

Chapter 3 lays out some of the methodological problems inherent in corrections research generally and, in particular, that involving criminalized women. The stranglehold of the 'psy-professions' (Ingleby 1983; Kendall 2000), which characterizes the penal enterprise, is examined in detail. Operational strategies and data collection techniques designed to address and overcome some of these challenges are discussed. Feminist methodologies are applied to further expose and deal with the subjectivities of social scientific research.

Chapter 4 begins to make sense of the data by looking specifically at women's pathways into prison – poverty, histories of physical and/or sexual abuse, histories of state controls, and defiance of gender norms – and draws important connections to the fallout of neoliberal policies that converge to bring women into 'conflict with the law' in the first place. Women's entanglement with other state control agents, such as foster care, welfare, mental health, and child protection agencies, prior to their entering prison are examined.

Chapter 5 explores the 'prisoning' of women by connecting time spent on the inside as an integral component of women's chances of 'making it' on the outside. Major categories emerging from this exploration include two-tiered prisons (federal versus provincial, formal versus substantive equality), criminalizing mental illness, and institutionalizing women. These discussions set the stage for connecting women's experiences with the criminal (in)justice system, most notably in identifying the important transitional links from prison back to the outside world.

Chapter 6 looks at the immediate and measurable transitions facing women upon release from prison. The practical realities of leaving prison require securing safe and adequate housing, searching for meaningful employment, and renegotiating interpersonal relationships. Managing these formidable goals is a major challenge in itself given the current political climate, which has seen a sharp increase in homelessness and a deepening of poverty for single mothers.

Chapter 7 focuses explicitly on women after prison. Key discussions related to transcarceration and social control are presented. Here, I look specifically at the differences and similarities between both groups of women (those who did and those who did not return to prison within a two-year period) in terms of staying out or, alternatively, going back into custody. The findings deal predominantly with the group of repeatedly criminalized women who have stayed out of prison and chronicle the direction of their lives post-incarceration. Structural forces that either facilitate or block women's bid to stay out of prison are given a critical look, and the shifting onto localized control systems and the layering of social controls is elucidated.

Finally, progressive policy recommendations are proffered to address the widening inequalities that contribute to women's criminalization in the first place based on the fallout from neoconservative and neoliberal policies of governance. The call is made for a broader vision (Wilson 1996) to avert our gaze from prisons as the policy solution to homelessness, poverty, mental illness, and abuse. The simple rationale is that it would be unnecessary to focus on prisoner 'reintegration' if women were empowered through a host of other social institutions and, therefore, could avoid the inhumanity and further marginalization of a prison sentence in the first place.

1 Penal Controls on Criminalized Women

The punishing community, far from encouraging reintegration and conformity, may instead be creating a parallel universe, reinforcing for some an embeddedness which takes for granted that the only way to behave is criminally.

Worrall (1997: 59)

Internationally, Canada is erroneously hailed as a leader among industrialized countries for both its ideological and substantive approaches to imprisoning women. Developments in this country over the past decade have seen a purported shift in penal philosophy that now masquerades as progressive policies for imprisoned women. To counter the notion of Canada as benevolent jailer, this chapter interrogates the discourse surrounding women's involvement in crime by deconstructing the language that dominates the management of women in Canadian prisons and moves towards a broader understanding of the forces that perpetuate an oppressive criminal justice system.

Resisting Language Used to Individualize and Pathologize Women's Crime

As a starting point to assessing the neoliberal climate (detailed in the next chapter), which has become more punitive, individualizing, and pathologizing of women, the very language used to describe women's involvement with the criminal (in)justice system[1] must be critically addressed. The deconstruction of language is much more than an exercise in semantics, because how we use language contributes to defining certain behaviours and actions by women (or men) to be a violation of a prescribed social order. Our use of language sets the most disenfranchised women in opposition to the very systems – criminal justice, social welfare, and mental health – that are oppressing them economically, socially, culturally, politically, and, ever-increasingly, medically. As Horii put it: 'To name is to know; to know is to control' (2000: 107).

These important discussions are posed early as I continually struggle with making sense of (and keeping up with) the myriad of terminologies such as women in conflict with the law, female offender, clients, inmates, facilities, and 'control talk' (including corrections, reintegration, rehabilitation, cognitive behavioural therapies, and assertive case management) that are used to describe women's encounters with their oppressors. Some of the leading feminist scholars who have begun this process of deconstructing the language used to camouflage women's entanglement with the criminal justice system are Comack and Balfour (2004), Horii (2000), Comack (1996), Faith (1993). Labels such as 'female offender,' 'women in trouble,' and 'women in conflict with the law' have all been used to individualize women's criminality. However, a term such as 'women in conflict with the law,' as Faith has noted, denies the fundamental inequality of the relationship ... one cannot simply be in conflict with power to which one is subordinate' (1993: 58). Use of the designation 'female offender' fails to take into account that only a small portion of those who offend get caught and only takes into account those whose offending behaviour has been criminalized. We have all offended at various times in our lives. Identifying which groups get singled out and punished (or which ones escape apprehension and penalization) for their offences leads to an understanding of the many axes of social exclusion.

Comack offers 'women in trouble' as a phrase that sensitizes the reader to the personal and legal troubles that women encounter: 'Troubles that emanate from women's particular locations within a society that is capitalist, racist and patriarchal' (1966: 12). Horii takes the analysis a step further in arguing that, despite the best intentions of reformers, 'a prison is a prison is a prison [and the] structure of authority that produces the oppressed and the oppressors alike is the *key* to understanding the problem' (2000: 107). Horii takes aim at the disguising of punishment under sanitized euphemisms that fail to tackle the underlying power structures of 'corrections': 'the language of the oppressor, those reams of rhetoric and countless nice-nellyisms that effectively mask the barbarity of imprisonment behind policies fronted by cardboard people and programs are tools of this structure which must be disabled. Overlooking the covert power of euphemisms becomes blind acceptance (ibid.).'

The need to pay critical attention to deconstructing oppressive corrections language is pressing. Moreover, language deconstruction by feminist academics and activists requires greater sustained attention in order to uncover the systematic processes that label women as deviants and offenders in the first place (Schur 1984). The myths and stereotypes that surround women's criminal involvement need to be dispelled so that the capitalist, patriarchal, and racist foundations of the penal system's treatment of women are exposed. Gendered power imbalances are but one of the axes of exclusion: 'Given that labels are culturally .invested with ideological significances, and applied with prejudice, it is best to avoid them. Certain women are criminalized, through social processes, and these women are then labeled female offender, delinquent, woman in conflict with the law, criminal or, most courteously, lawbreaker. When we recognize the contextual bases of illegal actions and the discriminatory nature of criminalization processes as applied to either men or women, and when we demystify labeled women by showing their diversities as well as the commonalities they share as women in a gendered power structure, we lose the need for labels, or for gendered stereotypes' (Faith 1993: 59).

Even a cursory analysis of women's encounters with the criminal (in)justice system makes clear that laws (and, by default, the entire reputation of the criminal justice system) are more precisely *in conflict with women*. The overwhelming preponderance of women's crime can be directly linked to social, cultural, economic, sexual, and political oppression in a society that negates women's work in the private sphere, undervalues women's work in the public sphere, and continues to restrict the full civic engagement of women through misogynous institutions. The criminal (in)justice system is just one of the systems blocking women's equality by criminalizing poverty, mental illness, past abuses, and race/ethnicity. In Canada, the criminalization of systemic inequalities is evidenced at all turns by the over-representation of Aboriginal women in prisons, the increasing criminalization of women diagnosed with mental illnesses, and the feminization of poverty that further oppresses a discrete group of women who already exist on the margins in society. Particular groups of women, on the basis of their race and/or ethnicity, poverty, mental illness, or age (youth and elderly) suffer disproportionate discrimination in a society that privileges an Anglo, middle-class, heterosexual, male value structure.

Language is an essential management tool used to regulate compliance and shift the onus onto the individual to account for her or his wrongdoing. Discussions on the retooling of the language used to describe women's experiences with the criminal (in)justice system are still in their infancy, but this should be a core area of concern to any serious feminist investigation.[2] The term *criminalized women*, therefore, is invoked to emphasize the social, economic, political, psy-entific, and cultural *processes* that coincide and contribute to the labelling of women as *lawbreakers* and *offenders*.

At the heart of this research lies the well-received assumption of the benevolent 'community.' The accepted, indeed taken-for-granted notion that the community can somehow provide an empowering environment for women that cannot be achieved in prison is highly problematic. This flawed logic is based on a number of key assumptions. First, there is a lack of consensus as to how community is defined. There is wide disciplinary and even intradisciplinary disagreement on the meaning of *community*, more often used in the vernacular to imply a distinguishable geographical space (McCold and Wachtel 1998). Sociologists generally, however, adopt a definition of community that is based on social relations (such as ties to family, work, and home) and point out that the boundaries between prison and the community are increasingly more difficult to discern in a neoliberal climate because of cutbacks, the medicalization of deviance, and the blurring of private versus public space: 'it is by no means easy to know where the prison ends and the community begins or just why any deviant is to be found at any particular point ... the term community treatment has lost all descriptive usefulness except as a code word with connotations of "advanced correctional thinking" and implied value judgements against the "locking up" and isolation of offenders' (Cohen 1985: 58).

The so-called community has become the site of offloading by the state and that further blurs the divide between private and public space. To survive, local organizations must count on state funding to maintain their operations, and thus, they subsequently become absorbed into the formal state apparatus. It becomes clear 'that a probable outcome of this blurring is ... the creation of a hidden custodial system, under welfare or psychiatric sponsorship, which official delinquency statistics simply ignore. This is the real, awful secret of community control. Not the old closely guarded secrets of the penitentiary (the brutality, the chain gangs, solitary confinement). These things occur in the community – and this is, by any measure, progress. The secret is a much less melodramatic one: that the same old experts have moved office to the community and are doing the same old things they have always done. Once again, we do not know what they are doing, not because they are hidden behind walls but because they are camouflaged as being just ordinary members of the community' (Cohen 1985: 65).

Community is a term invoked by governments, reformers, feminists, and academics, but seldom do these groups concur on its meaning. As Worrall maintains, 'the term community has become a thoroughly promiscuous word, attaching itself to almost any activity formerly regarded as a responsibility of the state' (1997:3). Community incorporates a host of state officials such as those from social services, child protection agencies, the criminal justice system, and mental health agencies doubling as agents for rehabilitation and reintegration. Moreover, the regulatory community for women represents another layer of enforcement and urged compliance in their lives. The myriad of state regulators continue to play a major role in women's lives post-release; the majority of women who have successfully stayed out of 'trouble' and therefore not landed back in prison are now being controlled by localized agents. This finding is not new (see Cohen 1985; Scull 1977; Carlen 2003; Blomberg 2003). The extended intrusion into the so-called private lives of women ex-prisoners is taken up by local agencies who receive their core funding from government sponsors and who are expected to do much more, with a whole lot less.

In keeping with language deconstruction, the vested interests and power imbalances tied into the notion of community are grappled with at an early stage in this book, for *community* has become a political vortex constructed by the state to satisfy its own organizational interests despite the lack of a clear and concise definition of the term: 'The "community" is an elusive concept that has been too easily appropriated by the state to engineer support for limited initiatives that fail to grapple with fundamental inequalities in corrections. This term is contextually determined and discursively constructed to satisfy organizational interests. Without reference to the context of power, the community concept has become a pretext for intervention and exclusion' (McCormick and Visano 1992: 287). There is widespread disagreement among policy-makers and the public about what community actually encompasses and very little empirical support that it is effective in meeting its intended goals of rehabilitation, cost-savings, and humanity. In practice, 'alternatives' are ripe with euphemisms, such as 'personal care homes,' 'treatment centres,' and 'assertive case management,' which effectively camouflage the reality of a precarious existence for the subjects of this

control. Nowhere is this more evident than in the shift to deinstitutionalize prisoners and those diagnosed with mental illness which is driven
by advanced capitalist market economies seeking to disaggregate social
control models that are far too costly; by the advent of the therapeutic
millennium and psychoactive drugs; and by an alleged concern with the
more humane provision of 'treatment' services on the outside (Scull
1977). Therefore, 'an apparently radical decarceration strategy ends up
only shifting custody from the state to local level and becoming a revenue sharing carve-up between local agencies' (Cohen 1985: 96).

Resistance strategies employed by the middle and upper classes to
housing the 'mad' and the 'bad' in their neighbourhoods ('Not In My
Backyard' syndrome[3]) have forced the situating of these makeshift halfway residences in transient and all too often decrepit urban locales.
Treatments under these conditions of restraint are no more empowering
than they are in the rightly criticized confines of the institution. From a
purely economic stance, reducing expenditures by means of deinstitutionalization means doing less with less. The so-called treatment services and housing arrangements made available to ex-psychiatric
patients and ex-prisoners are heaped onto the private sector, largely free
of state regulation and inspection and more often than not circum-
vented into conforming to state-based ideologies. It amounts to little
more than the 're-packaging of misery.' As Scull has pointed out, 'it is
scarcely surprising to learn that decarceration in practice has displayed
remarkably little resemblance to liberal rhetoric on the subject. Indeed,
the primary value of that rhetoric ... seems to have been its usefulness as
ideological camouflage, allowing economy to masquerade as benevolence and neglect as tolerance' (1977: 152). I will return to discussions on
the ambiguity and appropriation of localized agents to carry out the
control functions of the state in chapter 7.

Theorizing Women's Criminalization

In emphasizing the structural locations of women's criminalization,
two strands of feminist theory are advanced, socialist and standpoint.
Socialist feminism allows for the macro-level investigation of women's
socioeconomic position located along the axes of gender and class.
Standpoint feminism allows for the privileging of marginalized voices
as a way to resist entrenched, value-laden, and androcentric knowledge
claims. This gives way to feminist epistemologies as invaluable tools
for deconstructing these knowledge legitimation processes.

Socialist feminism emerged largely from dissatisfaction with the essentially gender-blind character of Marxist thought, which regards economic class relations as the primary source of women's oppression. To Marxist feminists, the material basis of women's marginalization and inequality lies in the fact that as a group women work outside the labour economy. Women's labour is in the home and is reproductive, not productive. Therefore, women do not create surplus value in the economy. For Marxist feminists, the oppressor is capitalism, which exploits women's labour. This over-reliance on economic class to the near-exclusion of gender relations to explain women's oppression is a pre-emptive feature of Marxist feminism. To overcome this inherent limitation, socialist feminists seek to expose the ways in which capitalism interacts with patriarchy to oppress women more egregiously than it does men (Tong 1998: 119). While concurring with the central thesis advanced by Marxist feminists that women's liberation depends on the overthrow of capitalism, socialist feminists maintain that capitalism cannot be destroyed unless patriarchy is also destroyed. Patriarchy is the key driving force behind women's oppression and is exercised and reinforced through such institutions as marriage, child-rearing, and sexual practices. Patriarchy is a 'set of social relations of power, in which men control the labor power and sexuality of women. It is this control – both in the home and in the labor market – that provides the material base of patriarchy' (Messerschmidt 1986: 32). Strategies for change, then, rest on the overthrow of patriarchal relations that would permit women's sexual autonomy and obliterate the 'oppressive nature of sexual and familial relations for women with their link to relations in the public sphere' (Daly and Chesney-Lind 1988: 538). While Marxism recognizes only labour in the productive realm, socialist feminism recognizes the inextricable and inseparable linkages between production and reproduction: 'Relations of production and reproduction have varied historically, but in contemporary society, relations of production take the form of capitalist class relations and relations of reproduction take the form of patriarchal gender relations' (Messerschmidt 1986: 28).

Socialist feminists recognize that familial reproduction and the nuclear family are as important to the needs of capitalism as production in the workplace (Chesney-Lind and Faith 2001). Moreover, it recognizes that patriarchy affects the ways by which men control women's productivity. Even turning back to agricultural societies, how the appropriation of labour by those with power over the subordinate group, in both productive and reproductive spheres, played out is well-documented (Messerschmidt 1986). Moreover, the appropriating group has '(1) defined what work should be done and how it should be performed, (2) benefited disproportionately from the labor (both productive and reproductive) of the subordinate groups, and (3) used the labor performed by the subordinate groups to consolidate and extend its control over those groups' (Jaggar 1983: 36). Socialist feminists differ from their Marxist predecessors in that they view women's interests as inherent in, rather than subordinate to, the working-class struggles. They recognize the gender factor as well as the economic factor in the division of labour and the distribution of criminalization. The sexual division of labour is key to a socialist feminist understanding of oppression.

Burstyn identifies three integral characteristics of the sexual division of labour in a capitalist patriarchy. First, the nature of labour performed by women and men is different; while men labour in the productive sphere, women labour in both the productive and reproductive spheres. Second, 'normative heterosexuality [is] the major psycho-sexual organizing principle' of capitalist patriarchy; the sexual division of labour, 'divides the sexes into two mutually exclusive categories, creating gender, and enjoining heterosexual marriage for economic survival and biological reproduction.' Third, men control the 'economic, religious, political, and military systems of power in society' that perpetuate the capitalist patriarchy (1983: 53–6). Therefore, 'since the oppression of women and the working class is intimately related through the interaction of production and reproduction, the material base of society *as a whole* needs to be transformed to end that oppression ... [The call is for the creation of] a *socialist feminist society*, not just a socialist society' (Messerschmidt 1986: 31; author's emphasis).

A socialist feminist understanding of crime, therefore, stresses that crime occurs for both men and women in an economic and male-dominated context. Increased incarceration is tied to the larger prison industrial complex that reacts to social problems. The state, acting on behalf of corporate interests, has targeted a massive spending campaign on prisons. In turn, expenditures on welfare and education have dropped dramatically to fund the prison endeavour. Resources that were once used to support low-income women and their children and to enhance education efforts are now exchanged in favour of an expanding prison industrial complex for women.

Foremost in a socialist feminist analysis is the intermeshing of class and gender in the reproduction of a capitalist patriarchy. However,

socialist feminism has not gone far enough in integrating racial inequalities into the analyses. Patriarchy cannot be separated from capitalism, just as racism is integrally connected to oppression.[4] Further
criticism of socialist feminist theory is that it fails to account for agency,
that is, it exhibits an over-reliance on structural explanations (class-
based inequality, patriarchal subordination of women, and racial and/
or ethnic inequalities) to account for gender inequality. Socialist feminism, like its radical predecessors, is guilty of exclusivity in appealing
to a white, Eurocentric, heterosexual, middle-class group of women.
Such a false universalizing represents a distorted and privileged ver-
sion of 'truth': 'Thus the aim of feminism [should be] ... the establishment of feminist truth and becomes the deconstruction of truth and
analysis of the power effects which claims to truth entail. It is this rec-
ognition that knowledge is a part of power that underlines the claims
made by feminist postmodernists' (Smart 1998: 82).

One attempt to value knowledge at the margins that lacks official status as knowledge – legitimation – has been offered by proponents of
standpoint perspectives (Haraway 1996; Collins 1991; Smith 1987).
Dorothy Smith describes the connection between power and the legitimation of knowledge and the exclusionary nature of these processes: 'A
standpoint in the everyday world is a fundamental grounding of
modes of knowing developed in a ruling apparatus. The ruling apparatus is that familiar complex of management, government administration, professions, and intelligentsia, as well as the textually mediated
discourses that coordinate and interpenetrate it' (1987: 108).

Standpoint feminism relies on the notion that previous feminist
attempts to account for the intersectionality of race, class, and gender
have been deficient. The predominantly white and middle-class
women's movement (Chardonnay feminism), with its focus on gender
alone, essentially ignored the diversity of women's lives. The epistemological basis of feminist knowledge is, however, experience which is
'achieved through a struggle against oppression; it is, therefore, argued
to be more complete and less distorted than the perspective of the ruling group of men. A feminist standpoint then is not just the experience
of women, but of women reflexively engaged in struggle (intellectual
and political)' (Smart 1990: 80). The standpoint perspective privileges
position in gaining knowledge and understanding. One's position in
the social hierarchy potentially broadens or limits one's understanding
of others. Members of the dominant group have viewpoints that are
partial in contrast to those from subordinated groups who have greater

potential for fuller knowledge. Therefore, the only way that we can know a socially constructed world is to know it from within. But since our knowledge and perceptions about reality are shaped by our own unique experiences and how we interpret them, there is little or no possibility for value-free and objective knowledge.

Although standpoint feminism has much to offer in advancing knowledge deconstruction it has tended not to problematize masculinity. Many feminists recognize the importance of questioning what it is about masculinity that makes it the most important variable predicting criminal involvement. Hegemonic masculinity remains separate from, in opposition and superior to, femininity. However, in countering this criticism, Smart states that 'it is precisely because standpoint feminism in this area has risen from a grassroots concern to protect women and to reveal the victimization of women, it has not been sympathetic to the study of masculinity(ies). Indeed, it would argue that we have heard enough from that quarter and that any attempts by feminists to turn their attention away from women is to neglect the very real problems that women face (1990: 81).' Given the claim by feminists that we need to deconstruct gender, it is important to take account of this theoretical shortcoming, while at the same time heeding Smart's warning of not falling into the androcentric trap of taking men's experiences as the starting point of analysis and, subsequently, the standard by which women are evaluated.

There is no monolithic feminist criminology. There is, however, a multitude of viewpoints about women's subordination and their subsequent involvement in crime. As Boritch has pointed out, 'many feminists now take the position that to adopt any single definition of feminism, or approach to gender and crime, would limit the development of feminist perspectives in criminology' (1997: 78). Some feminists have moved more towards an examination of social control issues that propel women into crime (e.g., Daly and Maher 1998; Miller 1998), and others argue that we need to move away from the traditional confines of criminology altogether (e.g., Cain 1990; Smart 1990) on the ground that it restricts an examination of central questions about women and fails to liberate them from their oppression.

Smart contends that the 'core enterprise of criminology is problematic, that feminists' attempts to alter criminology have only succeeded in revitalizing a problematic enterprise, and that, as feminist theory is increasingly engaging with and generating postmodern ideas, the relevance of criminology to feminist thought diminishes' (1990: 70). She regards criminology as something of a sideline for feminist thought, with feminist criminologists risking something of a marginalized existence – marginal to both criminology and feminism (ibid.: 71). This challenges the modernist assumption that once we have the theory (master narrative) that will explain all forms of social behaviour, we will also know what to do and that the 'rightness' of this doing will be verifiable and transparent (ibid.: 72).

There is now a large body of feminist empiricist literature exploring claims to objectivity, grand theory, and the deconstruction of knowledge (see, e.g., Keller 1996; Smith 1987; Haraway 1996; Hartsock 1998). Feminist empiricism encapsulates a body of work that criticizes the claims to objectivity made by mainstream social science. It points out that what has passed for science is, in fact, the world perceived from the perspective of men, what looks like objectivity is really sexism, and the kinds of questions that social science has traditionally asked have systematically excluded women and their interests. Feminist empiricism claims that a truly objective science would take account of both genders. Therefore, knowledge in the everyday world is socially constructed, and the political, economic, social, and cultural contexts of knowledge generation, acquisition, and transmission must be taken into account. Whose knowledge comes to be accepted as the 'truth,' who has a voice in the creation of knowledge, and what the intervening factors are that play into the legitimation process of knowledge, such as the 'relations of ruling'[5] (Smith 1987) are important tenets of feminist methodologies. In this regard, issues surrounding who decides what becomes acceptable as knowledge in a particular spatial, temporal, and cultural context are paramount.

Before knowledge becomes accepted in the everyday world it has to undergo a 'legitimation process' that results in an 'official' decision being made as to its legitimacy. If the decision-makers (patriarchal capitalists) perceive some knowledge to challenge the status quo, an approving assessment of this threatening type of knowledge might be withheld as a consequence and it will not be recognized as legitimate. This leads to marginalized knowledge, and many creators of such marginalized knowledge have come from oppressed groups, such as women and non-whites. Conversely, much legitimized knowledge has come from members of the dominant groups who have some affiliation with the ruling class (Clement and Myles 1994).

Feminist writings on the value-laden and androcentric bases of scientific knowledge, such as those of Evelyn Fox Keller (1996), have pioneered the deconstruction of knowledge claims and have argued for the inclusion of feminist ways of knowing in the experimental design of (social) scientific research. Keller discusses the relationship between knowledge and power and notes that both are intermeshed – knowledge is about legitimacy and legitimacy is about power. More recently, feminists critiques of the objectivity and legitimation of science (Keller 1996; Haraway 1991) have entered the criminological discourse (e.g., Naffine 1996; Smart 1990; Scraton 1990).

Feminist epistemologies attempting to deconstruct and expose the value-laden assumptions of social/scientific knowledge have also sparked feminist writings in the area of research methodologies. Issues grappling with power relations inherent during the research process have been an integral part of discussions and debates. Nevertheless, there is still a lot of work to be done in this area. Feminist discussions of research have yet to describe fully the complexity of power and struggles with subjectivity in research (Ristock and Pennell 1996). Feminist methodologies and epistemologies are inextricably linked to subsequent theory construction. Before we can theorize from data, we must understand the knowledge construction and legitimation processes that guide our research. We need to recognize the subjectivities of the researcher and take account of the power that is institutionalized in a masculinist form throughout all aspects of the criminal justice system: 'if academic discourse and its patriarchal context is to be challenged it needs to be considered within a broader framework of how ideas gain currency, become transmitted and eventually become institutionalized or consolidated as knowledge' (Scraton 1990: 15). It is from this vantage that feminism offers its greatest potential to transform the criminological discourse: 'Feminists have carried out the more conventional (but necessary) empirical work of documenting sex bias within the criminal justice system. Feminists have questioned the scientific methods deployed by criminologists, as well as their highly orthodox approach to the nature of knowledge. Feminists have engaged with criminological theory, across the range, questioning its ability to provide general explanations of human behaviour. Feminists have provided an abundance of data about crime from the viewpoint of women (to counter the more usual viewpoint of men), and feminists have also helped to develop new epistemologies that question the very sense of writing from the perspective of a woman (or, for that matter, from the perspective of a man)' (Naffine 1996: 4). Alongside knowledge deconstruction based on power relations, gender needs to be a central focus of inquiry in criminology: 'The deeper understanding which studying women and crime bring to criminology ought to result in a paradigm shift. Gender, and hence the explanations of gender-related patterns, should become central. That has clearly not happened. Instead, there is now a vast store of material on women offenders, women and crime and women and penology which is, no doubt, taken seriously and widely used for its impact on women. But the importance of gender for criminality is only perceived in terms of victimology ... A central question therefore remains about gender: how can it be built into criminology to play the central part in explanation and analysis it must?' (Heidensohn 1987: 24).

In examining the myriad of factors that propel people into crime and, likewise, the social control mechanisms in place that restrict criminal involvement we need to move beyond the boundaries of criminology and look towards the broader social, economic, political, and cultural issues that contribute to the construction of gender in society. We need to critique the androcentric knowledge-making and legitimation processes and similarly critique criminological theories that exclude women from their research and analyses and then argue objectivity and scientific rigour. An understanding of feminist epistemologies is presented here to make the transition to later deconstructions of penal 'knowledge' as privileged claims-making that is based on the experiences of white, middle-class men.

Penal Industrial Complex

Canada, like other industrialized countries, is locking women up at rate that should be criminal itself. We have witnessed an almost twofold increase in the number of federally and provincially sentenced women over the past decade. It is instructive to note that even in a neoconservative climate, the number of men admitted annually to federal custody for a first federal offence has decreased over the five-year period 1997–8 to 2001–2, while the numbers of women sentenced in the same category have increased during this same period (Canada, Solicitor General 2002). Women are most notably affected by neoconservative and neoliberal strategies that have waged wars on drugs and welfare in Canada. In particular, racialized, young, and poor women, as well as women with mental disabilities[6] are over-represented in prisons (Canadian Association of Elizabeth Fry Societies 2003b). All of this is taking place against the backdrop of 'woman-centred corrections.' To locate the source of this incongruency, the broader economic forces at play that make prisons a profit-making industry need to be explicated.

The corrections enterprise in Canada, as in all industrialized nations, amounts to big business. The expansion of the prison industrial complex is marked by increasing incarceration rates and, subsequently, exorbitant amounts of money that contribute to the maintenance of this industry (Sudbury 2004; Davis 2003; Hallinan, 2001; Christie 2000; George 1999). As Davis has noted, 'the term "prison industrial complex" was first introduced by activists and scholars to contest prevailing beliefs that increased levels of crime were the root cause of mounting prison populations. Instead, they argued, prison construction and the attendant drive to fill these new structures with human bodies have been driven by ideologies of racism and the pursuit of profits' (2003: 84). Understanding the prison industrial complex insists on 'understandings of the punishment process that take into account economic and political structures and ideologies, rather than focusing myopically on individual criminal conduct and efforts to "curb crime"' (ibid.: 85).

Stemming from neoliberal ideologies and corporate globalization, the prison industrial complex represents the growing move towards privatization of prisons (Van Wormer 2003), corporate interest and exploitation of 'human misery markets' (Hallinan 2001), the erosion of social programs and offloading of government responsibilities onto individuals (Comack and Balfour 2004), and the racialization of prison populations (Sudbury 2004). The racial composition of U.S. prisons today rivals the proportion of black-to-white prisoners during the era of the Southern convict lease and county chain gang systems.[7] Similar rates of selective criminalization exist in Canada, with the disproportionate number of Aboriginals behind bars in this country (Jaccoud 1992).

The corporatization of prisons and the clandestine profit-motivated agendas behind prison expansion form a growing area of critical interrogation; however, it is noteworthy that in classifying the prison industrial complex the subsidiary business of localized 'corrections' has been overshadowed. As we know, 93 per cent of all prisoners are eventually released (Petersilia 2003). Profit-making from the penal enterprise is an ongoing corporate windfall outside the prison. Furthermore, given that almost half of all prisoners under state or federal jurisdiction in the United States are African American (Davis 2003) and almost one-third of women prisoners in Canada are Aboriginal, it can be seen that entire communities are wiped out by the penal industry. Returning from prisons to neighbourhoods that are characterized by poverty and retrenched inequalities means that criminalized populations remain under the effective control of corporate and racist agendas, and they continue to be excluded from society (Young 1999). By virtue of having served time in prison, these groups are further marginalized by their experiences of prison, removal from families and kinship supports, and denial of civic engagement.

Canada is by no means exempt from this mass embrace of the penal industrial complex and is increasingly following the lead of American multinationals in the business of locking people up. In 2003–4, for example, the annual penal expenditures federally in Canada totalled an estimated $1.5 billion. This represents an increase from 1995–6 (in both current and constant dollars) when the expenditures amounted to an estimated $1.1 billion. Likewise, provincial and territorial penal expenditures are massive, totalling approximately $1.3 billion in 2003–4 (Canadian Centre for Justice Statistics 2005). The majority of penal expenditures are consumed in the maintenance and operation of prisons. In 2003–4, the annual cost of incarcerating a woman was approximately $150,000 while locking away men ranged anywhere from about $75,000 to about $110,000 per annum, depending on the level of security. The costs of monitoring a prisoner on conditional release[8] however, have dropped dramatically lower, averaging about $20,000 per annum (Corrections Service Canada 2005). Horii has eloquently argued that the 'correct' description for the 'business' of the Correctional Service of Canada (CSC) is the Penal Services Among Canada (PSAC) whereby the direct connection between the Public Service Alliance of Canada (PSAC), the largest public service union in the country, parallels the clear link between jails and jobs (2000: 107).

Prisons for federally sentenced women in Canada have undergone significant overhauls in the past decade. The first of these so-called changes took place in 1990 with the appointment of a federal task force to investigate the conditions of women in prisons: *Creating Choices: Task Force on Federally Sentenced Women* was designed to help remedy the problems of inadequate research on women's prisons and to suggest alternatives to incarceration. The mandate of the task force was 'to examine the correctional management of federally sentenced women from the commencement of their sentence to the date of warrant expiry, and to develop a policy and a plan which would guide and direct this process in a manner that is responsive to the unique and special needs of this group' (*Creating Choices* 1990: 88).

The findings of the task force profiled several important areas of concern including overclassification,[9] geographical dislocation and isolation, separation from families, inadequate programming, cultural ignorance (particularly with respect to Aboriginal healing practices), and the high incidence of self-injurious behaviour at the Prison for Women (P4W). The task force recommendations included the call for the wider use of conditional release sanctions for women. Unfortunately, as has been the case with so many recommendations originating from task forces and commissions, they have not been acted upon in a manner consistent with their stated philosophies. It can be argued that the plight of federally sentenced women in Canada has worsened with the decentralization of prisons and the concomitant resources now required by already cash-strapped local groups to provide regional services. The laudable intentions of local groups are often misappropriated and integrated into a prison rationale to sustain funding. The result is the mangling of penal ideology into a more powerful penal rationale favouring punishment as the guiding principle. Subsequent human rights violations by the state are pervasive against the backdrop of a legitimation process whereby the supposed adaptation of a woman-centred approach is usurped by penal ideology and substantive practices that further advance a law-and-order agenda.[10]

Certainly, failings of the task force's recommendations are evidenced at the local level. Proposed developments of release strategies adhering to the principles of the task force, for example, have been lost. Moreover, I argue that even the rhetoric of a woman-centred penal approach has never made it past the prison gates. The focus on empowerment, meaningful and responsible choices, respect and dignity, supportive environments, and shared responsibilities[11] is clearly absent in the community blueprint.

Despite the ongoing neglect of localized strategies emanating from the task force, four in five criminalized adults under the authority of the federal prison system in Canada are under institutionalized control outside prisons. Considerable debate and controversy have accompanied the widespread development of so-called community sanctions. Proponents argue that 'community corrections' provide a more humane approach to punishment, are cost-effective, and facilitate rehabilitation, while opponents argue that community options are widening the net of punishment and control and are merely supplements to incarceration (Cohen 1985). Despite opposing views, local initiatives continue to expand with little empirical evidence supporting their success. What research is available is based on the experiences of criminalized men, while the experiences of localized penal initiatives for women are consistently ignored or considered to be the same as their male counterparts (Maidment 2002).

Since the late 1960s, community corrections have become a major part of the criminal justice apparatus in Canada. There is now an endless range of localized programs available, including everything from community service orders and probation to boot camps and electronic monitoring. Although the number and type of localized options have expanded, so too have the numbers of participants involved in these programs. 'Correctional personnel or systemic net-widening'[12] and 'offender net-widening'[13] are in evidence, as the number of prisons has grown alongside the number of women under localized controls. In Canada, five new federal prisons for women have been built since 1995 at an estimated capital cost of $54.6 million[14] (Correctional Service Canada 1995). Prison operations for women were regionalized in the 1990s, and they now operate to maximum capacity in Truro, Nova Scotia; Joliette, Quebec; Edmonton, Alberta; Maple Creek, Saskatchewan; and Kitchener, Ontario. As an obvious consequence of new prison construction and regionalization, the number of staff needed to work inside these prisons has expanded correspondingly.

Debates surrounding the success of localized initiatives are not new; they have been reported in the criminological literature for decades (Solomon 1976; Scull 1977; Rothman 1980; Christie 1981; Chan and Ericson 1985; Cohen 1987; Matthews 1987; Carlen 1990; Blomberg 2003). The crux of these debates can be broken down to reflect a longstanding practice of viewing local sanctions as 'alternatives,' thus implying imprisonment as the norm. These so-called alternatives are included in a scale of punishment with prison as the toughest comparator (Jousten and Zvekic 1994: 2). All other custodial and non-custodial sanctions are measured in direct relation to punishment meted out by the prison: 'Imposing punishment within the institution of law means the inflicting of pain, intended as pain. This is an activity which comes in dissonance to esteemed values such as kindness and forgiveness. To reconcile these incompatabilities, attempts are sometimes made to hide the basic character of punishment. In cases where hiding is not possible, all sorts of reasons for intentional infliction of pain are given ... None of the attempts to cope with intended pains seems, however, to be quite satisfactory. Attempts to change the law-breaker create problems of justice. Attempts to inflict only a just measure of pain create rigid systems insensitive to individual needs. It is as if societies in their struggle with penal theories and practices oscillate between attempts to solve some unsolvable problems' (Christie 1981: 1).

Nils Christie calls for the advancement of alternatives to punishment (1981). In doing so, the rationale is to inflict as little pain as possible and reduce to a minimum the perceived need for infliction of pain for the purpose of social control. To this end, 'social control [is] genuinely decentralized; systems of expertise and knowledge [are] broken up; the euphemistic language of "treatment" [is] abandoned; and the state take[s] on a minimal role' (Cohen 1985: 254). Viewing local alternatives through this lens shifts the focus from the prison and the concomitant urge by well-intentioned reformers to situate the range of non-custodial alternatives along a continuum of punishment that tend to use them as alternatives to one another, rather than as alternatives to imprisonment (Carlen 1990). Punishments are cleverly disguised by euphemisms such as 'community alternatives' which garner support from those concerned with cost-savings, on the one hand, and appease 'get tougher' neoconservatives, on the other.

Monetarily, the 'decarceration' movement is itself tied primarily to economic considerations by the state in an attempt to control the escalating costs of incarceration. However, local initiatives have not been effective in meeting their economic goals but, rather, have contributed to a substantial growth of the criminal justice apparatus. This has resulted in increased penal costs (Chan and Ericson 1985). Consequently, a major concern surrounding an increased use of localized programs for women is precisely that it would bring more women into the penal apparatus (net-widening) under stricter and more onerous state controls (net-strengthening) (Maidment 2002).

It is understood that both parole and probation are back-end sanctions and, therefore, do not contribute to net-widening per se; however, emergent penal trends are enhanced by using electronic surveillance technologies (e.g., electronic monitoring devices and global positioning systems) and are becoming ever more intrusive. Use of these technologies strengthens the penal net and further undermines efforts for 'community' re-entry (Micucci, Maidment, and Gomme 1997). The term *net-widening*, then, expands outside the criminal justice system to include other state-run and local initiatives that control the lives of former prisoners, including mental health organizations, social services, child protection, and non-profit service agencies. Net-widening is closely aligned with *transcarceration* in its fundamental blurring of public/private system boundaries.

Behavioural restrictions imposed on criminalized individuals at a local level make such so-called alternatives less humane than they were designed to be. Local programs tend to reproduce the very same coercive features of the system that they were designed to replace. This book explores the blurring of community boundaries as this relates to women prisoners and ex-prisoners. Through the voices of women ex-prisoners we can see that it is ever more difficult to distinguish the break between state-run programs and those administered by local agencies who must stick close to the control talk and behaviouralist agendas of the state in order to sustain their funding. The community can be as repressive a site for punishment and control as the prison. Underlying penal rationales that fail to depart from the traditional goal of punishment, neoliberal governance strategies that wage wars on the poor, women, and racialized groups, neoconservative policies that call for even tougher crime control tactics, and economic motives that view communities as a means of meting out cheap so-called justice usurp even the most benevolent of intentions.

2 Sociopolitical Context of Criminalizing Women

The problems of recidivism and post-release mortality have less to do with the character and actions of individual women than with the intolerance and neglect shown toward women prisoners, their particular circumstances, and their needs.

Davies and Cook (1999: 272)

It is imperative to situate the constrained structural and economic parameters within which women generally are forced to operate on a daily basis, because we know that conditions of poverty are amplified once women exit the prison. It is illogical to expect an economic improvement for a woman who has just served a prison term and been effectively removed from the labour market for a considerable period. Therefore, broader structural forces surrounding women's criminality are canvassed through the lens of both neoconservative and neoliberal strategies of governance that have brought about a dismantling of the welfare state, an offloading of collective responsibilities onto the shoulders of individuals and families, and the construction of disorderly populations (Hermer and Mosher 2002). This broad focus is followed by discourse analysis surrounding the prevailing 'formal versus substantive equality' debate that pervades penal ideologies and determines the climate for further controls.

Neoliberal and Neoconservative Strategies of Criminalization

Critical criminologists (e.g., DeKeseredy and Schwartz 2004; Renzetti, Edleson, and Bergen 2001; Raphael 2000; Young 1999; Parent 1998) and sociolegal theorists (e.g., Daly 1994; Comack and Balfour 2004) provide a compelling analysis of the power of the state to reproduce a particular kind of order based on race, gender, and class inequalities. *Critical criminology,* a term which has been in use since the 1970s, is defined as 'a perspective that views the major sources of crime as the class, ethnic, and patriarchal relations that control our society [and] regards major structural and cultural changes within society as steps to reducing criminality ' (DeKeseredy and Schwartz 1996: 239). Critical criminology, based both in its origins and contemporary writings, draws heavily from the notion of exclusivity (Young 1999). An *exclusive society* in late modernity has been created and functions on three levels: economic exclusion from labour markets, social exclusion between people in civil society, and exclusion by the criminal justice system (ibid.: vi). An inherent feature of the exclusionary society is that penal institutions are used to govern marginality. Variations in these regimes occur according to their inclusionary or exclusionary agendas: 'Inclusive regimes emphasize the need to improve and integrate the socially marginal and tend to place more emphasis on the social causes of marginality. These regimes are therefore characterized by more generous welfare programs and less punitive anti-crime policies. By contrast, exclusionary regimes emphasize the undeserving and unreformable nature of deviants, tend to stigmatize and separate the socially marginal, and hence are more likely to feature less generous welfare benefits and more punitive anti-crime policies' (Beckett and Western 2001: 36).

Underlying an exclusionary regime are neo-liberal and neoconservative political ideologies. Neoliberalism is 'premised on the values of individualism, freedom of choice, market security and minimal state involvement in the economy. [It] marks a dramatic shift in emphasis from collective or social values towards notions of family and individual responsibility' (Comack and Balfour 2004: 40). The outcomes of neoliberalism have seen a 'retreat from any professed commitment to social welfare. Instead of formulating policies and targeting spending on programs that would meet the social needs of the members of society (education, health care, pensions, social assistance), governments now focus on enhancing economic efficiency and international competitiveness. With the "privatization" of responsibility, individuals and families are left to look after themselves' (ibid.). The political ideology behind a neoliberal agenda 'argues for a survival-of-the-fittest reliance on market forces. The state should get out of the way of the forces that decide which regions, and which people, prosper and which don't. The only assistance the state should provide are "incentives" to work. The policy results of these views is a dramatic shrinking of the social safety net' (Martin 2002: 92).

Neoconservative policies, in tandem, shift the focus towards a law-and-order agenda. Policies targeting the underclass have become a governing tool in the arsenal of a neoconservative regime. In Ontario, for example, 'A central aspect of how the ... government has successfully carried out neo-conservative reforms is through its ability to construct "disorderly people." Squeegee kids, welfare cheats, coddled prisoners, violent youth, aggressive beggars are part of a modern rogues' gallery that has been used by the Ontario government to justify sweeping changes in the public character of government. Disorder and the people embodying disorder have become a central resource of political power in Ontario, one that is produced and managed as an essential feature of neo-conservativism across a wide range of government activities (Hermer and Mosher 2002: 16). Neoconservatives argue that the family and the church should be the source of charity and support for the unfortunate. This shift towards singling out the poor and disenfranchised groups is not a new state strategy. However,

> what is new and radical about the type of disorder manufactured by the ... government is that it is intentionally designed to dismantle the welfare state. In other words, making up a disorderly set of people has come with an erosion of some of the central principles that have underpinned the democratic and equitable character of our institutions, diminishing the ways in which we are made to feel responsible for each other. And what is most disconcerting about this shift, ... is that it has taken place at the very sites in which the government is responsible for some of the most vulnerable and marginalized in our society – those with mental-health issues, the young, the poor and disabled, and a disproportionate number who are in correctional facilities. (ibid.: 16–17)

Social and criminal justice policy outcomes under both neoliberal and neoconservative regimes result in a weakening of social service provisions for the most vulnerable in our society and a social Darwinist approach to governing. The fallout from both neoconservatism and neoliberalism registers in an increased socioeconomic divide between the upper and lower classes:

> Under a neo-liberal fiscal agenda, for example, private security, policing and correctional services expand, and treatment and social services are

privatized, while public institutions face cuts and private charities remain the preferred means to deliver services to offenders and victims. On the other hand, in aid of a neo-conservative moral agenda, a law-and-order retributive approach to social disorder and dysfunction is offered to reinforce hierarchical/patriarchal social disorganization. The former claims to celebrate the autonomous individual and thus argues for the elimination of all but the most essential intrusions by the state onto freedom of choice and action, while the latter insists on a combination of punishment and the charitable 'rescue-and-reform' model for the few social services that survive.' (Martin 2002: 97)

This targeting of already disenfranchised and powerless groups in our society under a neoconservative banner is acutely evidenced by recent Ontario legislation that criminalizes youth who otherwise should be trumpeted under an entrepreneurial banner for their efforts to eke out a living on street corners and intersections offering a marketable customer service. 'Squeegee kids' have been hard hit under the Ontario Safe Streets Act (1999). The politics of exclusion have come down hard on youth: 'The act of censuring squeegee cleaning in Ontario can be interpreted as being part of a more global phenomenon. In other parts of Canada, and in the United States and England, recent years have been witness to more and more legal controls being targeted against the poor. The ever-expanding activities of the criminal justice system, persistent cutbacks to social spending, skyrocketing costs of housing in large urban centres and growing gaps of income inequality show us that society is becoming more exclusive ... The reaction to squeegee cleaning in Ontario is a clear example of how a marginalized and relatively powerless group are being squeezed to the point of exclusion' (O'Grady and Blight 2002: 39).

Neoconservative and neoliberal strategies have contributed to the offloading and dismantling of the welfare state, which, in turn, lays the blame squarely on the shoulders of individuals for their 'wrongdoings': 'Taken as a whole, the legislative framework, the policies, the practices and the accompanying discourse operate to construct the poor as persons who don't deserve to be in control of anything; rather they are persons who need to be controlled, disciplined and reformed by others. Single mothers in particular represent disorder, since they stand outside the structure of both the hegemonic nuclear family and often, the labour market. Welfare recipients, and especially single mothers, are constructed as persons who ought not to possess any expectation of privacy; they are in effect, cast as objects, to be reformed by the 'public' for the betterment of the 'public.' Thus privacy is preserved for others, for the economically privileged' (Mosher 2002: 49).

Single mothers existing on welfare have been demonized and stripped of any privacy rights under neoconservative government policies. The coveted divide between public and private space is eroded under this regime whereby targeted groups come under stricter enforcement and surveillance through mandatory drug and/or alcohol testing, unannounced home visits by welfare cops in search of violators ('spouse-in-the-house' rhetoric), and other draconian policies that violate citizens' rights to privacy. It is against this tide of neoconservativism that women are forced to negotiate a balance between their right to privacy and a dependence on the state for their livelihoods and the maintenance of their families. Failing to strike that illusory balance, women often find themselves in opposition to these structures and criminalization results. Entanglement in the criminal justice system brings with it a whole other set of contradictions and discriminatory treatment.

Formal versus Substantive Equality Paradigm

A plethora of research on criminalized women has developed over the past quarter century (Adler 1975; Simon 1975; Bertrand 1979; Berzins and Colette-Carrière 1979; Carlen 1988; Hamelin 1989; Faith 1993; Boritch 1997; Bertrand et al. 1998; Parent 1998; DeKeseredy 2000; Frigon 2001; Hannah-Moffat 2001; Chesney-Lind 2002; Carlen 2002; Kendall 2004). Strategies for advocating women's equality have been swayed by two predominant strands of feminist thought: formal equality and substantive equality. Formal equality theorists advocate sexual equality in all spheres, including the criminal justice system. Practically translated in prisons, this means that the range of programs and services available to male prisoners should also be made accessible in number and type to women prisoners. Informed by liberal feminist leanings, parity is achieved through gender-neutral standards. Formal equality is predicated on an assimilationist agenda under which 'members of oppressed groups (women, racialized people, people with disabilities, Aboriginal peoples, poor and working-class people, lesbians and gays, transgendered people) have been expected to direct their equality-seeking activities towards proving that they are the same as members of the dominant group' (Majury 2002: 104). Therefore, the onus is to demonstrate a likeness to the prototype (in this case male prisoners).

Critics of the formal equality model argue that women's structural locations are so acutely different from those of men that women require different treatment in the criminal justice system. Because equality is measured against a male standard, women will always come up short. Equality has been defined as rights equal to those of men, those of women are Other under the law and the human bottom line is always male. The result is a 'separate but equal' ideology that translates into glaring deficiencies in penal programming for women. Different for women has surely meant less.

Substantive equality theorists, therefore, reject the formal doctrine based on its inherent principle of relativity and its dissociation from a social rooting. The former criticism is based on the dependence of formal equality on a comparison group (male prisoners) and the lack of insight into the gendered realities that propel women into prison in the first place. Substantive feminists recognize these gender-based disparities as an expression of power. The adoption of a woman-centred corrections is grounded in a substantive framework; it attempts, at least in theory, to place women at the centre of penal planning and management and to elevate women's experiences to the forefront of inquiry. However, as we have witnessed through the implementation of the recommendations in the report *Creating Choices* (or the lack thereof on many counts), a well-intentioned woman-centred approach in theory cannot survive the overriding demands for punishment and security that are inherent to the prison regime (Hannah-Moffat 1995).

Canada the Benevolent Jailer?

Compared with men, women commit significantly fewer crimes. Consequently, a much smaller proportion of women are imprisoned. In 2003–4, in Canada 386 women were sentenced to federal penitentiaries compared with 7,308 men (Correctional Service Canada 2005). This proportion (5.28%) represents an increase from 2000–1, when the federal incarceration rate for women was 3 per cent (Canada, Solicitor General 2002). Women constitute a slightly higher proportion of those admitted to provincial and territorial institutions. In 2000–1, women represented roughly 9 per cent of admissions to provincial and territorial prisons in Canada (Canadian Centre for Justice Statistics 2002).

The majority of women's criminal activity is directly related to their disenfranchised socioeconomic status in society and has appropriately

been dubbed 'survival crimes.' Research shows that women's participation in property crime is linked to their disadvantaged position in
society. Many more women than men in Canada continue to be living
below the poverty line; dependent on welfare; unemployed or under-
employed in low-paying, semi-skilled jobs with few or no benefits; and
the sole supporters of children (Canadian Council on Social Development 2005). As a consequence of neoliberal social policies that rupture
the social safety net, especially for mothers on welfare, the concurrent
rapid increase in female-headed households, and the stresses associated with poverty, increasing numbers of women are being charged
with shoplifting, cheque forgery, and welfare fraud. The proportion of
poor children living with single or lone mothers has grown substan-
tially in recent years. In 1980, this proportion was 33 per cent, but by
2000 it had risen to 39.4 per cent (Statistics Canada 2001). Much of the
economic disparity between women and men is directly connected to
the fact that women constitute the overwhelming majority of single
parents. In Canada, four out of five lone-parent families are headed by
women, a proportion that has remained relatively constant since the
mid-1970s. Of these, more than half (53%) have incomes that fall below
the low income cut-offs (LICOs)[1] (Statistics Canada 2004).

Women continue to make up a disproportionate share of the Canadian population with low incomes. In 2002, women accounted for 55
per cent of all Canadians classified as having low incomes. The average
earnings of employed women still fall far below those of men. In 2002,
the annual estimated earned income of women was about $23,000,
which is far below the $36,000 average annual earned income of men,
including part-time workers (Human Development Index 2004). Table
2.1 outlines the unofficial poverty rates in Canada. Based on these calculations, an unattached person in St John's with an income below
$13,160 per year would be poor: no woman in this study had a total
income that reached this amount! In direct comparison with the LICOs,
table 2.2 shows the social assistance rates for both unattached individuals and lone-parent families throughout the province of Newfoundland and Labrador. Clearly, the annual incomes of single women and
single-parent families fall far below the low income cut-offs. Several
important stand-alone points are also identified in table 2.2. Most notably, average benefits for lone-parent families have not kept pace with
inflation rates; average benefits for unattached individuals have actually decreased since 1999; and the average duration of reliance on social

Table 2.1 Canadian low income cut-offs, based on population of manucipality, 2004

Family Size	500,000+	100,000– 499,999	30,000– 99,999	Less than 30,000	Rural areas
1	$20,337	$17,515	$17,407	$15,928	$14,000
2	$25,319	$21,804	$21,669	$19,828	$17,429
3	$31,126	$26,805	$26,639	$24,375	$21,426
4	$37,791	$32,546	$32,345	$29,596	$26,015
5	$42,862	$36,912	$36,685	$33,567	$29,505
6	$48,341	$41,631	$41,375	$37,858	$33,278
≥7	$53,821	$46,350	$46,065	$42,150	$37,050

Notes: This table uses the 1992 base. Income refers to total post-tax, post-transfer household income.
Source: Canadian Council on Social Development (2005).

Table 2.2 Social assistance rates for unattached individuals and lone-parent families in Newfoundland and Labrador, 1999–2003

	1999	2000	2001	2002	2003
Lone-parent and unattached (n)	29,300	28,930	27,480	27,205	27,900
Average benefits	$5,300	$5,400	$5,100	$5,100	$5,300
Average duration (months per year)	9.1	9.2	9.3	9.3	9.3
Lone-parent families (n)	9,255	9,085	8,485	8,150	8,175
Average benefits	$7,200	$7,300	$7,400	$7,300	$7,400
Average duration (months per year)	9.4	9.4	9.4	9.4	9.4
Unattached individuals (n)	20,075	19,850	19,000	19,055	19,725
Average benefits	$4,500	$4,500	$4,200	$4,200	$4,400
Average duration (months per year)	8.9	9.1	9.2	9.3	9.3

Source: Strategic Social Plan (2004).

assistance benefits has remained constant for lone-parent families while it has increased for unattached individuals. The overall picture is one of a deepening entrenchment of poverty levels among single-parents and their families.

Further analysis of the particular economic situation in Newfoundland and Labrador points to consistently high rates of unemployment and underemployment. Table 2.3 provides recent unemployment figures for the Canada and the provinces. Newfoundland and Labrador has unemployment rates more than twice the Canadian average and by far the highest among all the provinces.

Table 2.3   Annual unemployment rate (%), Canada and provinces, 1997–2003, seasonally adjusted

Province	1997	1998	1999	2000	2001	2002	2003
All	9.1	8.3	7.6	6.8	7.2	7.7	7.6
Newfoundland & Labrador	18.6	18	16.9	16.7	16.1	16.9	16.7
Prince Edward Island	15.4	13.8	14.4	12	11.9	12.1	11.1
Nova Scotia	12.1	10.5	9.6	9.1	9.7	9.7	9.3
New Brunswick	12.7	12.2	10.2	10	11.2	10.4	10.6
Quebec	11.4	10.3	9.3	8.4	8.7	8.6	9.1
Ontario	8.4	7.2	6.3	5.7	6.3	7.1	7
Manitoba	6.5	5.5	5.6	4.9	5	5.2	5
Saskatchewan	5.9	5.7	6.1	5.2	5.8	5.7	5.6
Alberta	5.8	5.6	5.7	5	4.6	5.3	5.1
British Columbia	8.4	8.8	8.3	7.2	7.7	8.5	8.1

Source: Canada, Statistics Canada (2004)

Furthermore, certain groups of women are over-represented amongst the ranks of the poor, based on race and/or ethnicity. For example, the average income of Aboriginal women is $6,000 less than that of other Canadian women or of Aboriginal men, and women are much less likely to have employment (Hadley 2001). In light of these economic disparities, it is not surprising to find that a disproportionate number of female prisoners in Canada are Aboriginal. While Aboriginal women constitute just under 3 per cent of the adult Canadian population, in 2003 they represented almost 30 per cent of federally sentenced women (Canadian Human Rights Commission 2003). Time and again it has been noted that 'Aboriginal women and their children suffer tremendously as victims in contemporary Canadian society. They are victims of racism, of sexism and of unconscionable levels of violence against women. The justice system has done little to protect them from any of these assaults. At the same time, Aboriginal women have a much higher rate of over representation in the prison system than do Aboriginal men' (Manitoba, Aboriginal Justice Inquiry 1991: 475).

An overwhelming proportion of criminalized women are single mothers. Although some prisons for women purportedly permit visits by children, efforts to encourage and enable such visitation are often lacking. Many women never see their children during their incarceration because the distance between the prison and their home makes travelling between sites impossible. On the federal scene, the regionalization of prisons for women in Canada was intended to help alleviate the geographical separation between women and their children. Arguably, however, the regionalization of prisons has had little impact on most prisoners and their families, who continue to experience the difficulties involved in being located several hundred kilometres away from one another. Indeed, regionalization has amounted to 'equality with a vengeance' (Chesney-Lind and Pollock 1995). For most prisoners' families, travelling to Kingston, Ontario, or to a neighbouring province is equally difficult, if not impossible – financial reasons restrict or prohibit visitation.[2] The establishment of regional prisons may well be more problematic for women who can no longer seek support for the claim that being located several thousand kilometres away from their home communities is a major problem for them during their period of incarceration. There was very little public sympathy or institutional support for such claims when women were centrally located in Kingston, much less at their present locales, geographically closer to their homes.

In terms of accessing programs and local services, the regionalization of prisons has worsened the situation for federally sentenced women. For instance, the decision to locate the Atlantic regional prison in Truro, Nova Scotia, was a political manoeuvre that did nothing to enhance the range of services available to women incarcerated there. Undoubtedly, the prison would have better served the needs of the prisoners if it had been located in a larger urban centre with greater access to programs and services.[3] Provincially, the problems created by the distance between home communities and jails pose similar challenges for the families of women prisoners, given that most Canadian provinces have only one jail for women serving provincial sentences – making the opportunity to remain in close contact with family members and children non-existent.

As a culmination of the ongoing discrimination of women on the basis of sex, race, and disability, and despite the purported enactment of reforms as recommended in *Creating Choices* (Task Force 1990), in May 2001 the Canadian Association of Elizabeth Fry Societies (CAEFS), in conjunction with a number of other equality-seeking women's groups,[4] launched a complaint to the Canadian Human Rights Commission: 'On the grounds that the manner in which women prisoners are treated is discriminatory, [and] contravenes several of the prohibited grounds articulated in s. 3(1) of the Canadian Human Rights Act. CAEFS is concerned about the discrimination on the basis of sex that is faced by women throughout the system. In addition, we are very concerned about the discrimination on the basis of race that is the particular experience of Aboriginal women and other racialized women, as well as discrimination on the basis of disability that is experienced by federally sentenced women with cognitive and mental disabilities' (CAEFS 2003a). Based on these submissions, the Canadian Human Rights Commission (CHRC) undertook a broad-based review of the treatment of federally sentenced women on the grounds of gender, race, and disability. In December 2003 the CHRC released its report, finding that women prisoners continue to endure systemic human rights violations in the federal penal system and calls for a more gender-based approach to custody, programming and reintegration for criminalized women.

The CHRC report sets out a number of guiding principles in relation to the treatment of federally sentenced women that are consistent with human rights' laws, including (1) women prisoners have a right not to be discriminated against and a right to correctional services that are as effective as those offered to men; (2) equality must be based on the real needs and identities of women inmates, not on stereotypes and generalizations: the CSC must see as its duty the promotion and protection of women's human rights and this means that the CSC must take into account that some of the reasons that women offend, their life experiences, and their rehabilitation needs are unique (CHRC 2003).

The CHRC report put forth nineteen recommendations for action, the most prominent of which are: a security classification scheme should be created specifically for criminalized women, one that does not conflate issues of risk and need; harm reduction measures should be implemented to deal with addictions issues; resources should be allocated to deal better with mental illness issues; low- and medium-risk women should be accommodated in prisons with appropriate levels of security; responses to the rehabilitation needs of women should be impoved; provision should be made for appropriate and adequate housing, local programs and services; and release options for women. The findings of this report on paper are encouraging; however, cautious optimism must be exercised, as many of these same recommendations were made in earlier reports, including *Creating Choices* (Task Force on Federally Sentenced Women 1990), the Arbour Commission report (1996), the Public Accounts Committee report (2003), and the Auditor General's report on the reintegration of criminalized women (2003), and have not been acted upon.

The human costs of women's criminalization far outweigh any monetary costs in terms of the impact that it has on the women and their children. The effects of criminalization are difficult to quantify and vary in degree from one woman to another; nevertheless the consequences of criminalization have detrimental effects on the well-being, mental health, and future life chances of all former prisoners and their immediate families, especially their children. The personal costs associated with criminalization also extend to society as a whole. For example, the imprisonment of single mothers places an increased demand on the need for foster care services. Research shows that the majority of children of incarcerated women are placed in temporary foster care unless alternate arrangements can be made with other family members (Shaw 1994; Boritch 1997; Watson 1995; MacLeod 1986). A study conducted in England and Wales found that 90 per cent of fathers in prison left their children in the care of their spouses while only 23 per cent of mothers in prison could do the same (Shaw 1994). Child care is undoubtedly a concern unique to women in prison.

Children of criminalized women face untold hardships, including the stigma associated with their mothers serving time, the effects of physical separation and loss of a parent, and the problems associated with the transient nature of foster care services: During the period of their mother's incarceration, children are often shifted in and out of a number of fostering arrangements which leads to further isolation and loneliness. It goes without saying that criminalized women themselves suffer tremendous hardships during their period of incarceration. Self-injurious behaviour, especially slashing, is very common amongst women prisoners. Most women who injure themselves have histories of childhood sexual abuse and adult violence (Filmore, Dell, and Elizabeth Fry Society of Manitoba 2001). A common institutional response to this self-injurious behaviour is the use of solitary confinement (Martel 1999). Other forms of reprisal by prison authorities have been the suspension or cancellation of visitation privileges.

Illustrations of the human tragedy of women's incarceration are all too prevalent in this country. For example, the (April 1994) prison riot in Kingston, Ontario, which resulted in the brutal strip-searching by an all-male emergency response squad of female prisoners at P4W brought the horror and cruelty of prison life into our homes. Media coverage let everyone see the inhumane treatment of prisoners by staff and led to the appointment of a commission of inquiry to investigate. The Arbour Commission's report (1996) was scathing in its call for reform of the present system of segregating women for long periods, of employing male riot squads in prisons for women, and of strip-search-ing women; it also called for financial compensation for those women who had been subjected to this inhumane treatment.

When examining statistical profiles, government-sponsored commis-sions and inquiries, and other secondary sources, it is far too easy to lose sight of the human costs of women's criminalization. But media attention surrounding the tragic death in Ontario of Kimberly Rogers in 2001 places the human costs in chilling perspective. In April that year Kimberly Rogers was convicted of welfare fraud for having received student loans while collecting social assistance. Under the Ontario gov-ernment's 'zero tolerance' policy for welfare fraud, anyone convicted of social assistance fraud (on or after 1 April 2000) was deemed perma-nently ineligible for social assistance (Income Security Advocacy Cen-tre 2003). In Kimberly Rogers' case, the welfare office determined an overpayment and she was automatically suspended from receiving social assistance benefits for three months. She was subsequently sen-tenced to six months house arrest (with no means to pay her rent); repayment of $13,468.31 (although she had no job); and eighteen months' probation; she was allowed out of her apartment only three hours a week (during a heat wave in Ontario). At the time of her con-viction, Kimberly Rogers was five months' pregnant and suffering from a number of medical conditions for which she required prescribed medication. When her benefits were cancelled, her Ontario Works pre-scription drug card was also cancelled.

On 14 May 2001 Kimberly Rogers launched an important case under Canada's Charter of Rights and Freedoms that challenged the constitu-tional validity of the Ontario Works regulations that cancelled her ben-efits after her conviction. Three months later on 9 August 2001, Kimberly Rogers and her unborn child were found dead in her swelter-ing apartment before her application could be heard. On 15 October 2002, a coroner's inquest to investigate the conditions surrounding her death began in Sudbury, Ontario. Two months later, the coroner's jury released a number of recommendations including elimination of the zero-tolerance lifetime ineligibility ban; assurance that adequate hous-ing, food, and/or medication be provided to persons serving a custo-dial sentence of house arrest; assessment of the adequacy of social assistance rates; establishment of a committee to develop a model for assessing whether cases of welfare fraud should be referred for prose-cution; and assurance that benefits for drug therapy for life-threatening conditions not be discontinued during any suspension of welfare benefits (Eden 2002). Kimberly Rogers is a tragic example of the fallout that can ensue from draconian state-sponsored policies that threaten the very lives of women and their children through the erosion of social and economic programs. The case of Kimberly Rogers also focuses attention on the futility of localized initiatives (e.g. house arrest) in the face of dire economic conditions, circumstances that are all too common in the experience of criminalized women.

In addition to the human costs of processing women through the criminal justice system, the financial price tag is alarming. In 1989, the year before the release of *Creating Choices*, 203 women were in federal penal institutions in Canada; by 2002 this figure had increased to 355, representing a 65 per cent increase in the population of federally sentenced women (Canadian Association of Elizabeth Fry Societies 2003b). As already noted, in 2003–04, the average annual cost of incarcerating a federally sentenced woman was estimated at approximately $150,000. As seen in Table 2.2, this figure represents an amount that is more than twenty times the annual benefits of lone parent families on social assistance – $7400 in Newfoundland. It has been convincingly argued by many feminist scholars that if women's poverty issues were adequately addressed there would be little need for existing women's prisons, let alone the future construction of more of them. Eliminating women's poverty would result in enormous savings for the state, not to mention that it would fulfil Canada's international human rights obligations, contained in the U.N. Convention on the Elimination of All Forms of Discrimination Against Women, the International Covenant on Civil and Political Rights, and the International Covenant on Economic and Social Rights (see Canadian Feminist Alliance for International Action 2003).

3 Stumbling Blocks to 'Corrections' Research

Focussing on the world from the perspective of the margins allows us to see the world differently and, in many ways, more authentically.

Kirby and McKenna (1989: 33)

Despite a decrease in the overall crime rate in Canada, the incarceration rate continues to climb steadily. Canada now ranks among the top five jailers in the Western world in incarceration rates (Correctional Service Canada 2005). The numbers of women incarcerated in Canada have been steadily climbing, and the province of Newfoundland and Labrador is no exception to this trend. In 1997–8, fifty-six women were sent to prison in Newfoundland and Labrador, representing 3.9 per cent of all prisoner admissions. In 1998–9, that number was eighty, representing 5.3 per cent of the total custodial population[1] (Newfoundland and Labrador, Department of Justice 2001). In 2000–1, the proportion of women prisoners again climbed, reaching 8 per cent (Canadian Centre for Justice Statistics 2002).

The province has one provincial prison for women, the Newfoundland and Labrador Correctional Centre for Women (NLCCW), which is a medium-security prison located in Clarenville, 175 kilometres west of St John's; it is the only prison in the province for women, including those on remand who are awaiting a court appearance, those receiving provincial sentences (under two years), and low-security prisoners who are serving federal terms and held under the Exchange of Services Agreement (ESA)[2] (Newfoundland and Labrador, Department of Justice 2001). The NLCCW opened in Clarenville in April 1996, retrofitted from a minimum-security men's prison. From 1982 to 1996, the NLCCW was situated in Stephenville on the province's west coast (725 kilometres from the provincial capital). Prior to 1982, women were warehoused in a wing of the men's penitentiary located in St John's (*Evening Telegram*, 6 May 1995). The NLCCW has space for a maximum of twenty-two women, who come from all areas of the province, including remote locations in Labrador.

The plight of criminalized women in the province has come under scrutiny because of the lack of space, poor air quality and ventilation, inadequate medical attention, and the growing numbers of women prisoners who have mental health needs (Monster 2000; Rossiter 2001). There has been considerable pressure on the provincial government to address the concerns of criminalized women, although response to date has been minimal. Stemming from this public awareness campaign, a chapter of the Elizabeth Fry Society was launched by a coalition of women's advocacy groups (*Western Star*, 10 May 1997; *Express*, 16 November 1994). Relocating the prison closer to St John's (in 1996) was regarded by senior provincial bureaucrats as a way of dealing with some of these problems. Similarly, non-custodial sanctions were touted as remedial measures to deal with this situation. In 1994, an electronic monitoring program was implemented, with a major goal being the inclusion of more women into that program. While the frequency of conditional release and probation dispositions has increased in the province, the numbers of women in prison continue to swell.

The historical lack of attention and services provided to criminalized women in Newfoundland and Labrador is the result of the same set of conditions that exist for women across Canada including their small numbers in comparison with men, and remote prison locations with inadequate resources to address the growing issues of women's poverty, mental illness, and substance abuse. Reports have surfaced from the courts that show that women are *requesting* federal sentences in lieu of the lesser provincial term of two years less a day[3] in order to have access to 'treatment' services and counselling programs that are only available, albeit in a limited fashion, at federal penitentiaries. This is an alarming reflection of the dire state of provincial prisons, given the scathing indictment by the Canadian Human Rights Commission (2003) regarding systemic human rights abuses in federal prisons for women.

Peculiarities and Subjectivities of Recidivism Scales

A cornerstone concept of corrections is predicated on the theory of risk management. Actuarial attempts to predict the likelihood of an individual reoffending have gained enormous currency in the Canadian penal enterprise (Ross and Gendreau 1980; Gendreau and Ross 1987; Andrews 1989; Bonta, Pang, and Wallace-Caprettaz 1995; Gendreau, Goggin, and Little 1996; Blanchette 1997; Andrews and Bonta 1998; Motiuk and Blanchette 1998). Underlying the logic of risk management is the theory of 'cognitive behaviouralism,' which 'assumes that a person's thinking or cognition affects his or her emotions and behaviour ... [and that therefore] behaviour can be altered by changing one's thinking' (Kendall 2004: 54). Cognitive behaviouralism in the penal context 'works on the assumption that offenders have faulty or deficient thinking which causes them to engage in immoral or criminal behaviour. Programmes, therefore, aim to "remoralise" or "ethically reconstruct" offenders by teaching them to think "pro-socially"' (ibid.: 56). Rooted in the work of Canadian psychologists Don Andrews and James Bonta at the 'Ottawa School,' risk prediction scales such as the Level of Service Inventory–Revised (LSI-R) have gained international success as 'part of an escalating focus on managerialism, efficiency, and accountability in correctional systems and a movement away from concern with individual cases' (Shaw and Hannah-Moffat 2004). Actuarial assessments satisfy a neoliberal agenda of responsibilizing individuals. As well, they provide a heightened measure of accountability for prison staff (Kendall 2004).

Andrews and Bonta (1998) have developed what they call a 'psychology of criminal conduct' (PCC) that is characterized by cognitive deficiencies. With cognitive behaviouralism at its root, this invention brought renewed promise to the fledgling rehabilitative ideal of the 1970s and 'introduced a technique which allowed for offenders to be governed in ways commensurate with neo-liberalism' (Kendall 2004: 79). Under the broad banner of 'cognitive skills,' the 'psy' disciplines have reinvigorated the notion of individual responsibility for criminal conduct and provided neatly prepackaged modules that can be delivered by prison staff to replace or reprogram an individual's faulty criminogenic thinking (ibid.). Practically translated, cognitive behavioural therapies designed to 'fix' antisocial thinking and therefore divert individuals away from their criminal lifestyles are inextricably tied up in recidivism scales as management tools.

Women (and by default men) who are the objects of these actuarial assessments are altogether excluded from the knowledge production that defines the parameters and outcomes of risk and/or need assessments and therefore the validity of recidivism prediction tools. To remedy the exclusion of criminalized women from the knowledge-making process, feminists advocate researching 'from the margins' as the modus operandi for researching by, for, and with women, thereby privileging women's own accounts of managing risk. The margins, as best described by Kirby and McKenna refer to 'the context in which those who suffer injustice, inequality and exploitation live their lives. People find themselves on the margins not only in terms of the inequality in the distribution of material resources, but also knowledge production is organized so that the views of a small group of people are presented as objective, as 'The Truth.' The majority of people are excluded from participating as either producers or subjects of knowledge' (1989: 33).

So it is that I depart from some of the well-entrenched and taken-as-truth knowledge claims about women and their encounters with the criminal justice system. One such sweeping and subjective claim is that of recidivism predictions. The most frequently used indicator of individual successes and, by default the overall performance of penal ideologies and substantive practices, is the use of recidivism rates. As Bonta, Rugge, and Dauvergne claim, 'knowledge of the recidivism rate of released inmates is important because it is one of many indicators of success of a prison system's attempt to reintegrate offenders safely back into the community' (2003: 1). According to their measurements (ibid.), the recidivism rate for imprisoned women is approximately 20 per cent, only half of which represents the commission of new crimes, while the remainder is related to technical violations (administrative breaches of release conditions).

Most women who are imprisoned are not high risk and do not pose a threat to public safety. They do, however, present a high degree of need based on histories of abuse, child care responsibilities, and emotional and/or financial dependencies on abusive male partners. The subject of risk-need classification has been well canvassed by policymakers and academics alike (see Feeley and Simon 1992; O'Malley 2000; Chan and Rigakos 2002; Hannah-Moffat and Shaw 2003). In the case of criminalizing women, the 'hybridization of risk and need factors' has resulted in 'a substantial slippage between the concepts of risk and need.' The resulting hybridization of risks and needs can lead to the identification of a 'multitude of unrelated risk factors that in and of themselves provide no foundation for systemic rehabilitative interventions' (O'Malley 1999: 18). The term *need* then is both vacuous and enabling. It is a category that can be deployed to either extend the arm of the state or to reinstate welfare-based techniques of rehabilitation, which have an extensive history of medicalizing and pathologizing women's deviance' (Hannah-Moffat and Shaw 2003: 60–1). The conflation of women's needs as risk markers has led to the overclassification of women prisoners. In turn, the provision of services required to assist women in dealing with their needs hinges on androcentric and culturally insensitive risk-management schemes that are wholly deficient in responding to the needs of criminalized women (ibid.).

Recidivism scales as a tool for accurately measuring program outcomes are quite problematic, and there is no single measure of recidivism that does not carry with it certain disadvantages. The various measures that have been used all have serious shortcomings in terms of what they are purporting to measure and what they actually do measure. Most outcome measures rely on rearrest or reincarceration data, both of which are problematic in that they count someone as having committed another crime when in fact that person has not. An overwhelming majority of parole revocations result from technical violations of the conditions of release. In 2003–4, only between 1 and 2 per cent of federally sentenced women on conditional release were returned to prison for the commission of a new offence (Canadian Association of Elizabeth Fry Societies 2005). Therefore, failure to report monthly to a parole officer or violation of a curfew is counted in the same category as, say, breaking and entering. Recidivism rates simply do not distinguish between the types of crime that cause people to be returned to custody. Breach of probation falls into the same category as armed robbery in terms of tallying success or failure.

Another problem with recidivism rates is the cut-off period that is used to determine success. Most recidivism calculations use two years from the date of release as the typical cut-off mark. Therefore, if an individual makes it past two years without a return to custody that individual shows up in official statistics as a success or non-recidivist. This arbitrary time period is problematic for obvious reasons, most notably its subjectivity. Before designing a research project that focuses on criminalized women and their strategies for staying out of prison, therefore, it has first been necessary to grapple with a conceptual understanding of how success is to be defined. It was recognized at the outset that perceptions of success are highly subjective and vary widely depending on who is doing the defining. It was expected then that women would have quite a different definition of success than would prison officials. For instance, a woman entangled in the criminal justice system for most of her adult life would conceivably have a radically different view of success than that expressed by the officially sanctioned recidivism rates. It is critical, therefore, that women be given every opportunity to locate and name their own success and/or failure in the criminal justice system.

This 'official versus marginal knowledge' conundrum became quite evident during the pre-testing of the Research Guide (see Appendix). The corrections knowledge-legitimation processes and outcomes are unilaterally imposed on women who lack input and consensus concerning the factors that are used to predict recidivism. One of the women interviewed, for example, clearly defined herself as a success based on the fact that she had remained out of the system for one month. Given her extremely high level of institutionalization (twenty-five years spent cycling between prisons and psychiatric hospitals), she proudly proclaimed accomplishment during her most recent release by setting herself up in her own apartment. Her reasons for going back inside had nothing to do with the official risk characteristics (dynamic and legal factors). Rather, she felt that prison was now her 'home' and life on the outside was 'too scary.' This is quite different from the so-called success indicators of recidivism proffered by criminal justice policymakers.

Operationalizing Success

Based on the above peculiarities and subjectivities of recidivism scales, an official definition of *success* poses operational barriers. Indeed, adherence to official designations was *only* operationalized during the sample selection stage of my research. That is, the selection of a group of women who had not been reconvicted following a two-year period with a comparative group who had gone back into custody during this same period. At the outset, the strict adaptation of the two-year cut-off was employed in keeping with official definitions by Correctional Service of Canada and provincial justice departments. Because penal data-keeping at both levels of government adheres to the two-year mark as the official measure of recidivism, I opted at the data-selection stage to subscribe to this definition only to ensure a degree of uniformity (which in itself is problematic). Once the total sample was selected and matched, I departed from any reliance on official measures to characterize success.

Notwithstanding the problems of defining recidivism, adhering to feminist methodologies of researching from the margins (Kirby and McKenna 1989) allowed the women whom I interviewed to define their own success. Again, the imposition of any one particular definition was confined to the sample and selection stages *only* of my research. After the sample selection process, it was left entirely to the women themselves to characterize their own successes and/or failures. The balance of the research, then, centred around 'researching from the margins,' where the concern is 'how research skills can enable people to create knowledge that will describe, explain and help change the world in which [women] live' (Kirby and McKenna 1989: 33). As Stanley and Wise have poignantly ascertained, 'we need to reclaim, name, and re-name our experience and thus our knowledge of this social world we live in and daily help to construct, because only by doing so will it become truly ours, ours to use and do with as we will' (1983: 205).

Applied Feminist Methodologies

This research relies on two primary data sources. First, a Statistical Package for the Social Sciences (SPSS) database containing the sociodemographic history of all women sentenced to prison in the province of Newfoundland and Labrador during an eleven-year period (1990–2000) was accessed (n = 359). Second, in-depth interviews with two groups of *repeatedly criminalized* defined as having more than four criminal convictions (n = 22) were carried out over a nine-month period (January to September 2003).

A database providing the socioeconomic overview of the total provincially and federally sentenced female population for the period 1990 to 2000 was accessed first.[4] It was discernible from this database that the number of sentenced women in the province during this period stood at 359 (Rossiter 2001). This database was compiled from a review of the files of all criminalized women in the province. Selected social, economic, and health variables were constructed and placed within an SPSS data file for subsequent analysis. The eleven variables so constructed include: age, education, occupation, offence, length of sentence, reported psychiatric problems, previous incarceration, marital status, type of admission, ethnicity, and reported alcohol and/or drug problems.

This database was instrumental in locating and matching both groups of women who were interviewed. From here, it was determined that the total number of women deemed to be repeatedly criminalized stood at twenty-four, based on a major defining criterion that included only those women who had more than four prison admissions during the sampling period.[5] In fact, most of these women had significantly more than four prison admissions with several women having as many as twelve readmissions. From this total number ($n = 24$), eleven women were tracked for participation in this study.[6]

The number of repeatedly criminalized women, as identified above, who agreed to take part in this study ($n = 11$), were matched by a further sample of repeatedly criminalized women who had not managed to stay out of prison following a two-year stint on the outside ($n = 11$) (based on nine of the above-noted social, economic, and custodial variables contained within the SPSS database). The variables constructed to account for reported psychiatric problems and reported alcohol and/or drug problems were excluded for the purposes of sample generation for my study. Following the production of a comparative sample of women who have stayed out with those who had been consistently returned to prison, I matched the identification numbers from the SPSS database to the women's names. Semi-structured interviews were subsequently conducted with both groups of women ($n = 22$).

Before finalizing the 'Research Guide,' a pre-testing of the draft instrument was conducted with two women who were selected from each group. Given the dearth of literature exploring women's experiences of localized release and therefore an absence of prior research that could potentially have guided and identified important areas of focus for the study, it was important to pre-test the interview schedule and elicit feedback from women concerning the issues that they identified as affecting their perceived success or failure in staying out of prison. The exercise of pre-testing the instrument proved invaluable in targeting key areas and contributed to a much broader understanding of the overall lives of criminalized women. Given my adherence to correctional discourse, I had not originally conceived that women's prior life experiences outside the criminal justice system would play such a prominent role in shaping their subsequent encounters with the law. The 'layering of social control' theme was formulated at the pre-testing stage. Pre-testing is critical in keeping with the tenets of feminist methodologies (e.g., voice, reflexivity, positionality), whereby women are given every opportunity to frame the central focus and direction of the research in all areas that *they* identify as important. Following the initial pre-tests, the interview schedule was completely overhauled to reflect the areas of importance and concern that were identified by the women themselves.

The data were manually coded, as opposed to relying on a computer software package. Despite an implicit assumption that computer-managed analysis is by definition more algorithmic, systematic, and rigorous, and therefore better, this claim has little support. For example, the developer of Ethnograph, one of the more popular software programs, notes several pitfalls of qualitative software tools including: (1) an infatuation with the volume of data that one can deal with, which can lead to researchers sacrificing resolution for scope; (2) a reification of the relationship between researcher and data, wherein the researcher assumes that data are 'things out there' that can in a relatively simple and straightforward manner be discovered, identified, collected, counted, and sorted, thereby ignoring the fact that data are artefacts of complex processes of identifying, naming, indexing, and coding that, in turn, are shaped by theoretical and methodological assumptions; and (3) a distancing of the researcher from the data (Schwandt 2001: 28).

Manual coding allowed a high degree of interaction and familiarity with the data. It did not restrict the creativity, objectivity, and reflexivity that facilitated the development of key concepts and themes which emerged throughout the research process. Manual coding also allowed for the practice of 'hurricane thinking,' described by Kirby and McKenna (1989: 146–7) as one strategy for understanding the links between categories. It is a visual strategy for making sense of the emergent categories by using index cards moved around a core research question that is displayed in the centre of the page (the 'eye of the hurricane'). It allows the researcher to see patterns of relations that describe the data.[7]

The benefits of applying a reflexive approach to data analysis were realized early on in the data collection. It became very clear to me how taken up I was in listening to women's life histories and experiences (particularly their lack of family supports, histories of foster care, and histories of abuse) and how courageous and strong I considered these women to be. I marvelled at their survival strategies and began to query them on how they managed to overcome or, more precisely, how they sustained themselves in the face of ongoing adversity and hardship. This line of questioning was propelled by my own mindset at the time; I had just lost my father in the months prior to my conducting this research. For me, this major life event represented an unparalleled level of pain and anguish. I was very much struggling to keep the faith and enthusiasm that I had once taken so much for granted. Consequently, I was truly captivated by the strength and resiliency of these women who had endured such tremendous pain throughout their lives while still managing to cope and maintain a sense of themselves and the world around them. This theme, generated from my own personal reflections and positionality at that time, no doubt added another layer to the research that would not have been apparent had I not taken the time to position myself alongside these women. In turn, survival and resiliency became prominent themes in my research.

Feminist researchers attempting to extrapolate the voices of women on the margins shift the focus of standard practice from research concerned with men's agendas to locations and perspectives of all women. Throughout the research process, DeVault (1996) argues, it is imperative that we listen to the voices of our respondents and not selectively hear or document what fits neatly with our own subjective orientations. Failing to listen to the voices of our respondents runs the risk of recreating knowledge that suits our own personal, theoretical, or political agendas. In keeping with the presentation of women's voices at the forefront of this research, the data-analysis sections contain extensive use of direct quotations from respondents. I make no attempt to curtail what are oftentimes quite lengthy verbatim quotations if in doing so women's stories and experiences are captured in their truest form.

4 Getting In: Pathways to Prison

I do what I have to do. I am not all that criminal. I don't even think of myself as one anyways.

Rebecca

The next four chapters are taken up with data analysis and respectively include pathways to prison, the prisoning of women, transitioning from prison, and the persistence of control agents in women's lives upon release. To begin the criminalization trajectory, this chapter explicates women's pathways into prison. Doing so necessitates a review of some of the well-documented themes in the literature on women in prison generally and, in particular, as collectively identified by women in this study. These major categories include the poverty trap, coping with past abuses, histories of state controls, and defiance of gender norms.

To situate the analyses, a description of the sociodemographic characteristics of the total sample of women (n = 22) is presented. The average age for the entire group was thirty-seven years, and ranged from twenty-three to fifty years. This is slightly higher than the national averages for federally sentenced women, who tend to be younger than thirty-five. However, the average age of the population of adult federally sentenced women increased through the years from 1981 to 1998. The proportion of women over the age of thirty-five years increased from 31 per cent in 1981 to 51 per cent in 1998 (Filmore, Dell, and Elizabeth Fry Society of Manitoba 2001). In my sample population, the slightly higher age grouping may be explainable by the fact that both groups comprised women who had had lengthy histories of criminalization and therefore had been cycling in and out of prison for some years. That is, in my sample there were no first-time prisoners who could have lowered the overall age of the group. The education levels of respondents ranged from Grade 3 to high school completion with a mean of Grade 9. Not surprisingly given their low levels of education, the majority (59%) of these women relied on social assistance as their primary source of income. Their previous work histories were sporadic, and typically involved part-time, low-paying, 'pink-collar ghetto' jobs, primarily housekeeping, retail, food services, and elder care.

The majority (72.27%) of the women were single. There is no distinction made in this category between women who were single because they had never married, those who were widowed, and those who were divorced or separated. This categorization of single is that of the women themselves and is primarily an economic distinction. That is, the women defined themselves as single based on the fact that they did not rely on a partner for financial support. Finally, the overwhelming majority (90%) of respondents were of European descent.[1]

A comparative breakdown of both groups, using these same variables, reveals both similarities and differences. The average age of 'recidivists' and 'non-recidivists' was thirty-seven years for both groups. Education levels were slightly higher for the non-recidivist group (Grade 8 for recidivists; Grade 10 for non-recidivists). Although the majority of women in both groups relied primarily on social assistance, the 'no income' category was higher for the recidivist group – four of these women were incarcerated during the time of the interviews. All women in both groups were unemployed at the time of the interviews. The majority of women in both groups were single. Based on a comparative assessment of these six variables, there is very little difference reported between the two groups. Overall, sociodemographic differences tended to be insignificant. This is an important finding in and of itself. That respondents in both groups tended to be mirrored on sociodemographic variables points to more significant differences on other levels (these differences are elucidated in chapter 7, which deals with state and localized controls).

Consistent with national statistics, most of the women in this group were convicted of non-violent property offences. The most frequent offences were theft (27.2%), violations of provincial liquor acts (12.4%), assault (11.5%), and fraud (9.7%). There was little variation in this category between the two groups, with a slightly higher number of women charged with theft, fraud, and forgery in the recidivist category. This is an interesting finding in and of itself because one might expect greater variation based on type of criminal conviction. It is important to point out that despite moral panic invoked by the media, there has not been an increase in violent crimes committed by women. Official crime data in fact show a decrease in women's violent crime (Dell and Boe 1998). Furthermore, violence very often takes place in retaliation against years of abuse from a male partner (Neve and Pate 2005; Frigon 2003; Frigon and Viau 2000; Hattem 1991).

Women's pathways into criminal activity are remarkably similar, and usually rooted in socioeconomic considerations. Their lives are also characterized by long-standing histories of poverty, physical and sexual abuse, state controls, and defiance of gender norms. An in-depth exploration of each of these core variables forms the nexus of the remainder of this chapter.

Trapped by Poverty

All too often, the common denominator among criminalized women is a chronic cycle of poverty and dependence on welfare (Mosher et al. 2004; Burke 2002; Chesney-Lind 2002; Abell 2001; Ehrenreich 2001). Moreover, education, sex, age, and geographical location are strongly correlated to poverty. A recent study by Statistics Canada (2004) showed that workers with high school education or less are approximately three times more likely to live below the poverty line than are those with a university degree. Consistently, women are more likely to be employed in low-paying, part-time jobs than are men. Age of workers is also strongly correlated to the incidence and prevalence of poverty in Canada, as elsewhere. Twice as many women in the age group 16 to 24 years held low-paying jobs as women in age group 25 to 34 years. Compounding these demographic features that affect poverty rates, workers in the Atlantic Provinces have the highest incidence of low weekly earnings in Canada (ibid.).

Given that criminalized women typically mirror all of the demographic variables that account for an increased concentration of poverty, it is not surprising that poverty plays such a major role in women's criminal pathways. The criminalization of poverty has become an international trend for women. As observed by Wacquant, 'prisons of poverty' result from the increased over-reliance on the penal system to manage social insecurity and contain the social problems created by neo-liberal policies of economic deregulation and social-welfare retrenchment (2001: 401).

Canadians often hold the misguided perception that homelessness and poverty here are nowhere near the levels of our southern neighbours; however, as DeKeseredy et al. point out, the percentage of Canadians living in concentrated urban poverty parallels and, in many instances, exceeds that of our U.S. counterparts (2003: 2). In fact, Canada now has one of the highest rates of family and child poverty in the developed world, with an increase of 33.8 per cent in the poor population between 1990 and 1995 (ibid.: 5).

Evidence of the criminalization of poverty is being felt in all advanced capitalist societies where those at the bottom of the class structure are penalized by draconian state policies that target the poor. In Ontario, a lifetime ban on social assistance eligibility for anyone convicted of welfare fraud is one example of neoliberal strategies to penalize already disenfranchised populations, which are largely made up of single mothers and their families. The realities of poverty are most acutely felt by single mothers in their often-failed attempts to eke out a living on their meagre and wholly inadequate welfare incomes.

The number of single-parent families headed by women in Newfoundland and Labrador has grown by 13 per cent since 1991, and they now comprise roughly one-fifth of all families in the province with children (23,000). Undoubtedly, lone-parenting and the almost certain poverty that goes with it is a major factor in women's criminal pathways; this became a predominant theme throughout the interviews. Countless commentaries were made by women in describing these links. As one participant, Sarah remarked, social assistance benefits are so criminally low that they do even come close to covering the basic costs of living.

> Social services will not look after a single person. They give you dirt, shit money. You know it's not worth the paper it's wrote on for what you get ... They'll pay you up to $433 a month for rent. Electricity bill right now if you got a small child that child has to bath every night so that drives up your light bill. I have not seen an electric light bill under $200. Never in the winter months. You wouldn't get a flophouse for the money [they give you]. That's what's criminal.

For many women like Sarah, experiences of poverty are directly linked to failed attempts to provide for their children and the stressors associated with trying to manage the basic survival needs of a family:

> You are way below the poverty line living on social services and a woman to go out and have to buy extra fruits and vegetables and things for a child to eat to keep a child healthy they cannot do that on the budget they are

living on. I was getting $179 every two weeks. Now I was struggling with that. To buy your groceries and ... then you got a child going to school and they get in there and [you] can't afford to buy things. And then if someone comes around and things are stolen and says, 'Want to buy a pair of jeans for $20?' and they fit my daughter, yes, I'll take them.

Affordable housing presents an ongoing burden for low-income women. In a gender-based analysis of housing policy in Newfoundland and Labrador, the St John's Status of Women Council (2003) has pointed out that almost half of the tenant households in the province spend 30 per cent or more of their gross income on shelter and thus are classified as having a 'core housing need,' as defined by Canadian Mortgage and Housing Corporation (CMHC; 2003). Low-rental housing is in scarce supply in many areas of Newfoundland and Labrador. As this report notes, lengthy waiting lists exist for social housing; many rentals are in poor condition; there is a lack of short-term housing for abused women and their children as well as a lack of emergency shelters; and there is not enough accessible and supportive housing for people with disabilities and for seniors. Increasingly, single women and their young families are becoming part of the 'hidden homeless,' staying temporarily with friends and relatives ('couch-surfing') or in shelters (St John's Status of Women Council 2003: I). This burgeoning trend is reflected in an interview with Nicole, who personalized the affordable housing crisis in St John's:

> Most one-bedrooms wants $400 or $500 a month. They want damage deposits on top of that. Then they wants you to pay your own utilities. It's going to be costly to set up. It's still $350 or $400 for a bedsitting room. Three hundred dollars is the lowest I have seen and they still want a damage deposit. I've seen them around a little cheaper but they are all taken so fast. You're just getting a single room for all that money.

As Rebecca, a single mother of two, candidly put it, when you are forced to 'choose' between eating and paying rent few options remain.

> I have gone out on days and just stolen enough stuff to put food in the house for the kids. And I don't care. I will be ninety years old and if I don't have food in my house I will go and get it one way or another. If my kids are hungry, I am going to go and get it. Plain and simple. Just enough so I can feed the kids. I do what I have to do. I am not all that criminal. I don't even think of myself as one anyways.

Persistent commentary on the cycle of poverty and the lack of incentives to join the ranks of the working poor created by a substandard minimum wage was drawn by Charmaine in providing an economic rationale for her criminal involvement:

> The only real way I can explain it is like I said when I started out shoplifting it was for survival. But now ... like to go out and pay $90 for a pair of jeans when I can get them for nothing. I'd go out for half an hour and I'd have myself three or four hundred dollars and people are out there working their ass off for two weeks for that. Which is pathetic?

The dependencies created by social services are not lost on these women. For many of them, the availability of a drug plan through Social Services is an invaluable feature of welfare that they would not have if they were employed at minimum wage, which stagnates at $6.00 per hour, the second lowest in Canada (Human Resources and Development Canada 2005). Victoria provided an example of this trap and her cycle of dependency on welfare benefits:

> I am asthmatic. My inhalers is $100 and something dollars a month. I get a drug card through social assistance. I wouldn't be able to make it [without that]. That's why I am hanging on to this welfare. I want to work. It makes me feel better. I don't want to be on welfare for the rest of my life.

The feminization of poverty is an ever-increasing reality for women wage earners, who earn only 65.2 per cent of the incomes of their male counterparts (Statistics Canada 2004). Women are more likely to be concentrated in low-wage service jobs with little job security and few benefits, and they are over-represented in part-time and temporary work. Three-fourths of part-time workers in Canada are female (Canada, Statistics Canada 2004). The bulk of these part-time jobs are paid at the substandard minimum wage. Rebecca was well aware of this economic trap and sees little incentive to join the ranks of the ever-burgeoning working poor: 'There is no incentive to work for minimum wage. Maybe it's alright for a single person, living at home but it ain't no good for a family. I'd be worse off than I am now if I went that route.'

It is critical to point out that Aboriginal women are even more disadvantaged in the labour market. The average total annual income for Aboriginal women is $13,305 and it is $18,221 for Aboriginal men; the non-Aboriginal equivalents are $19,348 and $31,404, respectively (Canadian Association of Elizabeth Fry Societies 2004). Overall, Aboriginal people and lone-parent families are more likely than any other Canadians to be poor (Heisz and McLeod 2004).

Housing is an urgent need for poor single women across Canada. In Labrador, most of the housing in Aboriginal communities is in desperate need of repair; 3 to 10 per cent of homes lack bathrooms and running water, and up to one-fourth have unsuitable drinking water. Houses are smaller than the Canadian average, more overcrowded, and often shared by several families. Fully one-half of Aboriginal households in Canada are in need of core housing (Callaghan, Farha, and Porter 2002: 33–45). It is therefore no surprise that one Inuit woman I spoke with rejected a return to her home in Labrador, based on the rampant poverty and substandard living conditions there, none of which, as she clearly pointed out, would lend itself in any way to her reintegration. Poverty and the lack of affordable housing are major factors facing women upon their initial release from prison, when the stakes are highest in an attempt to 'go straight.' Poverty and core housing needs are themes that run throughout women's lives both before and after incarceration. Sadly, for some women, prison is the only viable housing alternative.

The psychological consequences of being poor are certainly not lost on these women. Poverty-related homelessness and its attendant despair are key determinants of illicit drug use (DeKeseredy et al. 2003). Many women, like Rachael, connect the emotional anguish of poverty to a decline in their physical and mental health:

> I guess being poor and not having a lot leads to overall depression ... and of course the depression leads to not having any money. So that's why so many people drinks and gets involved with drugs. Most drugs you can afford. Like a gram of weed that lasts hours and hours is only $20.00. And you stay so high that you don't really know if you are in the world and you are so happy. That is why people does it because you are so depressed you would rather go into another world than face the fact that they are on welfare, got no job, and everything seems to be falling apart.

Rachael is quoted at length here as she drew the links between self-esteem, poverty, abuse, and criminalization:

> When you are poor and you got a low self-esteem and most families who grow up in the welfare system, and I am not prejudice or targeting the

poor, but most homes you do not get a lot of healthy self-esteem. Eventually it comes to, when you don't have a good family background where you got a lot of love and support you go to drugs and eventually to relationships that are unhealthy because you don't care because you have such a low self-esteem, that someone paying attention to you makes you feel better. Whether or not they are dirt themselves or they beat you, to you that's good because you got that all your life so what is the difference now? You go drinking because you don't want to deal with the fact that your partner is beating you and you don't want to live with him and you are so scared to go home and then, of course, your drinking leads you back out into the world of doing criminal charges. It's all linked together. It is a chain. It is the poverty, then it's the self-esteem, then the drinking, and then the bad choices in relationships, your friends. Until you break one link on that chain you are always going to be doing the same thing.

In so many ways, these women are no different from the rest of the population who seek means to boost their overall confidence and self-esteem. Rachael described this quest:

It all goes back to self-esteem. I guess if you don't feel good about yourself, you are told you are gross all your life, that would cause you to go back, too. As for what keeps people out, it is difficult to say because each person is different. You take one person could have been raped, could have been beat up all her life. For me it was all emotional, well up until I met my partners and then it was physical. All this leaves scars. But the bottom part of it is poverty. That is the main contributing factor. If you got no money what do you do? If you got a family home you've got to provide for them ... It's pathetic. You go back and forth for robbing and [prostitution] to keep food and stuff for your kids.

The cycle of poverty is retrenched for many women by state-sanctioned impediments to climbing out of poverty. One of the strongest correlates to poverty is low levels of education. In 2004, families headed by individuals who did not graduate high school were at least twice as likely to fall below the low income cut-offs (LICOs) as those headed by people who had either a university degree or college diploma (Canadian Council on Social Development 2005). An oft-expressed desire to return to school and 'make something of oneself' is waged against the reality that in doing so you run the risk of being cut off from your only source of income, thereby making the goal of higher education unattainable. Jessica discussed the short-sightedness of the provincial government's fiscal policies with regard to the welfare trap:

> I had to quit school because Student Aid didn't come through. You are trapped there [on welfare] and you got no way out of it. You are stuck there and you are staying there. You are not getting anywhere else. If they sat back and said, okay fine, go to school and then maybe in a year or two they would be rid of me altogether. They don't look at it like that. There is no choice.

Unrealistic expectations when it comes to payment of fines are stumbling blocks for criminalized women already living in absolute poverty. Many women connected their prior convictions to their inability to pay the court-imposed financial penalties. Similarly, many women who would otherwise have stayed out of prison by all other accounts (that is, abiding by their release conditions) were awaiting upcoming criminal charges for default on payments of fines. Rebecca described the no-win position in which she found herself.

> They got it set up now that I am just waiting for a call, and then for someone to come and take me out of here and put me in jail for my fines. They give me a fine when I can't make ends meet here now. I've got fines that have accumulated over the years. Obviously I am out there making money because I don't have enough to live off. That is why I am out there. I don't have anything fancy around me. I don't even have a couch. Then they slap a fine on me. Sure they are only asking for me to come back. They give you a fine so that in a couple of years they can come back and get you again ... *I don't want to go back to prison but I can't afford not to.*

For women expressing a will to seek paid employment, even at substandard and low-paying service jobs, the presence of a criminal record is a major impediment to achieving this goal. Rebecca, in canvassing her options, pointed to this stumbling block 'There is no second chances here. You got a record no one will look at you. I can't even work at Tim Horton's or nothing because I am not bondable.'

Poverty also creates dependencies on male partners acting as the family breadwinners. In a recent study connecting abused women and their experiences of the welfare system in Ontario, Mosher et al. clearly denounced the neoliberal policies that drive women further under the control of their abusers: 'Women who flee abusive relationships and turn to welfare seeking refuge and support frequently find neither. Women's experiences of welfare are often profoundly negative ... They encounter a system that is less than forthcoming about their entitlements, and about the multiple rules with which they must comply ... They are often subjected to demeaning and humiliating treatment from workers within a system in which suspicion and the devaluation of recipients are structured into its very core. For many the experience of welfare is like another abusive relationship ... Disturbingly, the decision to return to an abusive relationship is often the "best" decision for a woman, in a social context of horrendously constrained conditions' (2004: v).

Staying in abusive relationships because of economic dependencies is echoed by several women in this study. Corrina described her structured choice in this regard:

> You wonder why everybody is scamming welfare. I'll tell you why. They won't let you get ahead at all. They won't give anybody a break. They get you in the rut and they keep you there. I am stuck here now fifteen years in an abusive relationship and I am sick of it. They try and keep you down ... [I] don't know what I would do if he [her partner] ever left me. I wouldn't be able to make it here alone without him. Otherwise, I'd be gone out of here for long ago.

Jamie recalled her attempt to flee an abusive relationship with two young children, the consequences of which landed her in prison:

> I had two kids to raise and I stayed in an abusive marriage because I had two kids. I did it for them, and I couldn't put up with it any longer when they got six years old. First time I got in trouble my husband went to court and filed a joint custody of one of them and wanted custody of the other one so I packed up the kids and took off.

For many women, departure from their parents' home when they are young results in an immediate entry into a heterosexual relationship in which the expectation exists for a man to provide financial support. This financial dependency on a male breadwinner is sometimes the only viable (and non-criminal) means of economic security. Resisting this route leaves many like Victoria homeless or turning to crime to support themselves:

> I did stupid stuff because I did not want to go back [to my parent's] home. I went to [university] for a while. I wrote cheques to have a place to stay in

B&B's and hotels. I didn't want to go home because my family background was so dysfunctional, and I didn't want to ask people for things. You don't do that, right? You are supposed to make it on your own. You're not supposed to screw up. So I wrote cheques. That was my first offence. After the first time going inside I learned about how to get prescriptions and stuff and then I started writing prescriptions, fraud, whatever I could. Then I moved in with him and things went downhill from there.

Charmaine found herself trapped in an unwilling dependence on a male partner for economic survival and knew what the reality facing her was if she left:

I wouldn't be able to live in this apartment if me and him split up because I definitely would not have enough to live off. I got to scam to get ahead. But I tell him to leave and then I am worse off. I would have only $600 a month to live, and that's not enough to pay my heat and lights. I am damn well not going into some bedsitter. No way. No. Then I would be out of my mind altogether.

The lack of legitimate opportunities created by absolute poverty leaves women with few options to support themselves and their families financially. This recurrent theme constrained many of the 'choices' women had to return to school to upgrade their education, to leave abusive relationships, or to secure safe and affordable housing.

Trapped by Abuse

The high prevalence of criminalized women with past histories of physical and/or sexual abuse has been well-documented in the literature (Filmore, Dell, and Elizabeth Fry Society of Manitoba 2001; Websdale 1998; Heney and Kristiansen 1998; Comack 1996). The Task Force on Federally Sentenced Women (1990), for example, found that over two-thirds of women interviewed (n = 191) had been physically abused as children or adults; over half of them (53%) had been sexually abused at some point in their lives. These figures are considerably higher among the population of Aboriginal women, where 90 per cent had been physically abused and 61 per cent sexually abused (Heney and Kristiansen 1998).

Comack revealed similarly alarming figures from a study of provincially sentenced women in a Manitoba jail, where an overall proportion of 78 per cent of women interviewed had been physically and/or sexually abused during their lifetimes (1996: 37). Again, the incidence of abuse among Aboriginal women, who comprise a disproportionate number of prisoners in Prairie prisons, was even higher (81%). Disturbingly high rates of abuse are evident among the women in my study. The links between trying to cope with abuses (past and present) and criminalization are clear. Kathleen described the never-ending torment of past abuse:

> I've got to start dealing with all the shit that is going on and deal with [childhood] sexual abuse issues. I'm thirty-three years old now and I can't take this anymore. I've got to get away from my common-law. I have left him before but he was in jail when I left him. He got a load of assault charges but he never gets any big time for it. A few months here and there in weekends and then I writes a cheque for $52.80 and I gets eighteen months. Figure that one out. The highest sentence he ever, ever had was thirteen months for assault. I don't know but it is just a homicide waiting to happen. I've got to get away from him [her common-law partner]. When I get out things are alright for a little while. Then things start to get abusive again and I start using [drugs].

Valerie connected her past abuse to her present-day addiction to prescription medications: 'I never dealt with my [sexual] abuse really. You forgive but you don't forget and you go on. I could not communicate. I keep it all bottled up and turn to the pills.'

For many women like Emily, their troubles with the criminal justice system began later in life, often as they began their journey towards a realization that the sexual abuse that they suffered was not a normal occurrence:

> I never drank until I was thirty-one [years old]. I had been doing stuff growing up but I hadn't realized until seven or eight years ago that that was a way of coping with things that happened when I was growing up. I never knew that. We were always taught that wrong was right and there was no arguing. To be raped and molested and all that was normal. Anybody who wasn't raped or molested there had to be something wrong with them.

For some women, once they began to deal with their past histories of abuse, their anger and hurt got redirected, and they began lashing out at various authority agents who had failed to protect them as young children. Jennifer described her entanglement with child protection services, and the anger she felt at the prospect of having her own child taken away because she was labelled 'unfit.' This led her to direct her rage and hostility at the police:

> I was told that my child was going to be taken away [by Child Welfare] as soon as it was born because of my history [in foster care and custody] ... If you are not given the freedom to talk about things it just builds up and builds up in your mind and eventually you are going to blow. And for me, unfortunately, I always took it out on people in authority. They were the only ones it seemed that were in a position to do something and they didn't. So I went in last time for assault of a police officer.

Another means of coping with the pain of abuse is to inflict harm upon oneself (Frigon 2001; Filmore, Dell, and Elizabeth Fry Society of Manitoba 2001). Self-injury is all too common among women prisoners. Heney found in her study of women prisoners that 59 per cent had engaged in self-injurious behaviour such as slashing, head-banging, starvation, burning, and/or tattooing. Heney has contended that 'self-injurious behaviour is a coping strategy that manifests itself as a result of childhood abuse, usually sexual abuse' (1990: 4). A lack of support systems and a sense of absolute powerlessness within a prison environment exacerbate the impulse to inflict pain upon oneself. The most fundamental dynamic underlying both child sexual abuse and incarceration is the structural distinction between the powerful and the powerless (Heney and Kristiansen 1998). Yvonne, who spent close to thirty years cycling in and out of prisons and psychiatric institutions, spoke of self-injury as a way of releasing the anger that she felt from having been sexually abused while under the 'care' of the state: 'I used to slash up and not even feel it. I had so much anger in me from all the abuse. When I used to slash up it used to relieve the anger and not even feel it. People didn't understand that release.'

Past abuse is oftentimes the marker for early state intervention in women's (and men's) lives. In Newfoundland and Labrador, for example, abuse of children in foster care by members of the clergy is all too clear in the public mind. Mount Cashel, an orphanage for young boys operated by the Irish Christian Brothers, was the site of physical and sexual abuse for more than a decade. Allegations of abuse by several young boys were reported to the police in 1975; however, these allegations were covered up by key justice officials. Nearly fifteen years later, a Royal Commission of Inquiry into the Criminal Justice System was established to investigate 'allegations of a cover-up in a police investigation of the sexual abuse of young boys living at the Mount Cashel Orphanage in St John's during the mid-1970s' (Hughes 1991). The victimization of these young boys was twofold, based on the long history of both physical and sexual abuse committed by members of the clergy and the subsequent state-church cover-up.

As we are reminded by the unfathomable horrors of the Mount Cashel scandal, when victims come forward to report their abuse it is often met with intervention and/or cover-up from so-called child protection officials and the start of a downward spiral of state-sponsored control in their lives. Jennifer described this pattern of intrusion as she talks about the foster care and mental health interventions in her young life as a result of *her* sexual victimization:

> My first suicide attempt was at eleven years old. We lived in this big old two-story house, and the boys were in one room and the girls were in another, but because there was no room in the girls' room for me I was put in the boys' room with the boys. He [live-in relative] used to come in and do a lot of things, and it wasn't until I made the suicide attempt he [abuser] was kicked out of the house. Then, of course, unfortunately child protection got involved ... I ended up in the Janeway [Children's Hospital]. I don't remember how long I was there but I was going back and forth for counselling for years. And then when I was fourteen I was admitted to the Waterford Hospital.[2] To this day I am the youngest person ever admitted to the Waterford Hospital.

The emotional burden of childhood sexual abuse leaves many women struggling to maintain any semblance of healthy adult relationships. As Olivia described it, her relationships with men have been complicated by the lingering effects of her sexual abuse. She still struggled with issues of sexuality and trust:

> I married when I was eighteen but it was kind of hard because it was kind of hard in a sexual way because he was trying to get my clothes off and going down around my crotch and stuff. Oh God. Thinking back then it was hard. I got in the bed with my clothes and all on and turned in. He was there like trying to turn me out and trying to get my clothes off. Oh, come on now. We just got married. But he didn't know [about my past sexual abuse] so I turned around and I told him so.

In the end, Olivia faced the additional trauma of discovering that her then-husband was sexually molesting family members. The discovery of this abuse eventually led her to violence towards this man. She explained:

When I was married I found out after seven years that my husband was a child sex offender. I was going to leave because it was two of my nieces that he was trying to get a hold to. Six months old and the other one was nine years old. He was caught feeling them up and everything ... So after I grabbed the gun and I went from there. I was going to shoot him and shoot myself ... Then a few years after all that I ends up with another guy I was going with for four years and lo and behold he was up on charges from [Little Island] for sexually assaulting kids. I said every man I gets involved with is always a child molester. I said every man I goes with in the past, no I am finished with men. I'm telling you. It seems like every one I am after going with is a child molester.

Olivia went on to talk openly about the pain she continues to suffer as a result of her horrific experiences of sexual abuse and her inability to reconcile the constant torment and 'psychological imprisonment.' She explained:

To tell you the truth I have been going in so many different directions, wrong directions. I am reaching for the bottle. I am reaching for someone to put their arms around me and say yes b'y I understands exactly what you are going through. What I wouldn't give. There is nobody on this God-earthly world who can ever take the pain away. It's just myself. I am the one that got to go to sleep and I am the one who got to face it the next morning. And to tell you the truth there is no bottle and there is no medication that can help that. This is the first time that someone has come in and it is actually being recorded what I am saying right now, you know. When I was younger I used to screech until my heart would drop right out of my soul. I wanted so badly for someone to hear what I was going through. That means a lot to me to have someone to hear me.

Olivia talked at some length about the implications of sexual abuse and the interplay it spins with state agencies:

I am after losing a lot because of that [sexual abuse]. I couldn't concentrate on learning when I was going to school. My mother was after putting me in four or five different schools. I remember one day she brought me in to the children's hospital to get tests done on me like you know brain scan and they couldn't find anything. Every night I used to go to bed and pee in my clothes. I used to wake up screaming and bawling that he [her abuser] would be there. In my dream he would be there after me in the dark and everything. Now today here I am at forty-six and you ask the guards. I will not go into that room by myself, and I will not go to sleep with that light off. The light got to be on ... To me, I am after turning a few times to the doctors in the hospital, but they didn't understand exactly what I was going through. I lost my education. I lost my home because I ended up in hospital a few times. They turn around, back in them days, they say I was unfit to look after a child. [They said I] was in the Waterford quite a few times. So they used that against me and took my child away. So then I turned more to the bottle and more to the pills and everything.

A large number of criminalized women have long-standing alcohol and/or drug addictions (Pimlott and Sarri 2002; Burke 2002). Well over half of women in prison report substance abuse or addiction concerns (Morash and Schram 2002). In my combined sample, the overwhelming majority cited alcohol or drug dependencies as a key factor involved in their criminal offending. Drug use is often a means of temporarily escaping the enduring realities of being poor. For many women, their realities are comprised of cyclical poverty, depression, and histories of abuse. Leanne characterized her connection between drugs and crime: 'Where I live [in public housing] there is a lot of people addicted to OxyContin[3]. 'My best friend is on them the past year. It is hard for me to stay off the drugs when I am living life like this. What have I got to look forward to?'

Turning to drugs and alcohol is often a 'damage control technique' (Comack 1996: 42) to help women cope with the pains of past abuse. Olivia described her attempts to medicate the hurt that she has endured and the lack of support received from so-called help agencies:

I did the wrong things. Facing the bottle. Facing pills. Taking four or five of this kind, this kind and that kind. And before you know it I am all loaded down with different kinds of pills. You figure that them two things, the bottle and the pills are your biggest friends. In the long run you are hurting yourself. And in the long run it don't make any sense because you say, 'Is they worth it?' You know. These people who hurt you, are they worth hurting yourself for? But in the meantime you just don't care. You got to turn to something because some of these people on the outside don't

ITEM ON HOLD

Title: Doing time on the outside : deconstructing the benevolent community / Madonna R. Maidment.

Author: Maidment, MaDonna R. (MaDonna Rose)

Call Number: HV 9507 .M315 2006

Enumeration:

Chronology:

Copy: 1

Item Barcode:

0 3 7 3 2 5 9 1

Item Being Held For

Patron: Alexandra D Butler

Patron Barcode:

3 0 0 1 7 5 3 9 3

Patron Phone: √ (250)499-5356

Hold Expires: 4/10/2011

Pickup At: Kelowna Circulation Desk

understand exactly what you are going through. Right. And then you feel hurt and you feel hate and you feel pain and everything. And it's times you got things in your mind that shouldn't even be there, right.

Olivia went on to make the point that no amount of deterrence tactics or punishment inside or outside the prison could take away the pain of her past abuse:

Even in here [prison] you figure that the pills are going to help you get through a day. To make you a little bit stronger. Now at first when you start doing it. Oh yes. It made me feel lots of energy to get up and go. You know. But the pills and the drugs they was the two things I turned to. Now some people turns to more things. People turns to cocaine, acid, and all kinds of drugs that would ease the pain. Just ease the pain a little bit. Just, you know, try and forget. Try and forget some things that happened in your past. Right. Just try and block it out. But next thing you know you end up doing something stupid and next thing you know you are in here. Like I said, I would be lying if I turned around and said to you there is no way in bloody hell that I will end up back in here, in this hell-hole. They could turn around, and they could put you in one of those fancy [restraint] chairs[4] they got in there, and they could beat the soul right clean out of you. But that's not going to change anything.

Addictions are closely tied to the commission of criminal activities. In Canada, 69 per cent of federally sentenced women have indicated that drug and/or alcohol has played a major role in their criminalization (Canadian Association of Elizabeth Fry Societies 2005). That is, either crime is a means to obtaining drugs or drug money or alcohol and/or drugs act as a catalyst for crimes committed under the influence. This pattern was borne out in my sample. Leanne described her pattern of criminal involvement and addictions:

I have been drunk every time I've done anything [criminal]. The first time I was incarcerated was a week before my seventeenth birthday. I turned eighteen in Whitbourne,[5] and I was eighteen when I came here [NLCCW]. It's all for shoplifting and two break and enters. It's all a big cycle of drinking and drugs and shoplifting with me. Needing to get money for drugs since I was seventeen.

Long before patterns of criminalization are established, young girls – many of whom have been victims of childhood abuses – encounter various other state control interventions stemming from their troubled family backgrounds. This layering of social control is discussed next.

Layering of Social Control Systems

One of the most striking commonalities for criminalized women is their often long-standing and layered experiences with state agents of social control *prior to* their period of incarceration. Most women who end up in penal custody have been under state control from an earlier age and usually for non-penal reasons (Carlen 2002: 126). These formal agents of control predominantly include child protection services, mental health agencies, foster care, and social services. In a study of thirty-nine women prisoners, Carlen found that nearly two-thirds had been through the 'care/custody mangle' (1988: 74). She points out that a disproportionate number of young women go directly from foster care into prisons. This pathway to prison is clearly present among those women in my study who had not managed to stay out of prison for any sustained period of time. Yvonne talked about her path from foster care into custody:

> Well where my criminal history comes in, it comes from my past abuse and where I have been in foster care all of my life and where I have been, physically, sexually, and mentally abused which led me into the criminal justice system. Getting involved with breaking the law. Because from my past abuse I had a lot of anger which causes violence which caused me to a lot of emotional issues which I had this negative attitude about life. I said to myself people don't care about me and I don't care about them. So anyway, from my past, all the abuse I have been through led me to a lot of anger. I was a very angry person. For a good fifteen years of my life I have been in and out of prison.

For many women, abuse began once they entered into fostering arrangements. Maggie told of her horrific experiences of state so-called care:

> I have been in foster homes since I was six months old. Every day I was beat and beat and beat. I was ignored. No communication. I would get beat around all the time. Then my foster father sexually abused me. I couldn't stand up for myself. I went through a hard time. There is a book out called *Suffer Little Children*[6]. I was in that home. I know first hand. If anyone across

Canada ever read that book you would know exactly where I am coming from and what I have been through. I was in the same foster home.

Having a long history of being bumped around from one foster home to another, Yvonne talked about her attempts to escape the abuse and how this was tied to subsequent criminal activity:

At sixteen, I start running away. Then I got into a girl's home and that's where it all started. The violence actually started in there. For the next fifteen years I was in and out, in and out, in and out [of prison]. I didn't care. The abuse numbs you. You can't think. What am I doing? You can't think. It takes a while to heal. It's a state of mind.

Christine described the effects on her of a number of social support systems that failed her as a youth including education, mental health, foster care, child protection, and the criminal justice system:

At eleven years old I was taken out of my parents' home. I was put in foster care. The first time I was in a juvenile jail I was twelve years old. It started off when I was mentally ill one time when I was in a foster home and I went out to K-Mart. I stole some products. A fifty-cent eye pencil I got caught with. I was supposed to write a letter of apology but I couldn't because I was dyslexic, and they couldn't understand that so they shoved me juvenile. I couldn't explain to them why I couldn't write the letter because I write backwards and I didn't know how to do the apostrophes and they didn't understand.

Admissions to psychiatric institutions are all too often a precursor of women's criminal pathways. As Valerie pointed out, going to prison was for her the lesser of two evils when weighed against the prospect of spending the rest of her life in a psychiatric ward:

I went into the youth centre in Pleasantville[7] for girls and boys when I was thirteen. I was in a psychiatric unit when I was eleven. I've mostly been in hospitals, institutionalized. I would go to court and they would put me in hospital on a normal ward. Whatever you call normal in there. So I got in trouble in B.C. [British Columbia] and they put me on a forensic unit. They wanted to do a report with the psychiatrist and I wouldn't do it because I knew what would happen. I would spend the rest of my life in a forensic unit.

Child protection agents play a pivotal role throughout the lives of many criminalized women. Either women had been wards of the state during their own childhoods or they had encounters with child welfare when mothers themselves. In Maggie's case, child welfare intervened in her young life as she was removed from her family home, placed in foster care, and subsequently diagnosed with a psychiatric illness. Because of her 'mental instability' child welfare agents deemed her 'unfit' to look after her own child:

> When I was eighteen I had my first child. They [Child Welfare] took my child away because I was in the Waterford a few times and they used it against me ... Then welfare turned around and took him away on me. I tried to get him back but no, no. They used the same thing on me as before. I was an unfit mother. I shouldn't have him and blah, blah, blah. Two days before Christmas child welfare came to my door and said your son passed away. Then I tried to commit suicide.

While under the control of the state, any act perceived to be in defiance of authority can have very serious consequences and often results in disciplinary action (Neve and Pate 2005). As Maggie described, her resistance as a young girl in open custody to those in positions of authority landed her further criminal charges and a persistent record of violence, for which she was subsequently classified as maximum security in the adult prison system:

> When they put me in open custody I done some violent acts at the juvenile jail. They were trying to put me in a suicide-watch cell to calm me down. And they were trying to rustle me to the cell, and so I hit them to get away from them. They charged me for when they were trying to rustle me to the cell, and I touched them and they took my clothes off and put me under suicide watch. So they charged me with that and I got months added on. If I was in open custody, I would say, 'I'm not fucking listening to you. You know, you're not my mother or you're not my father, so go to hell.' They would tell me to go to my room. I would say, 'I'm not fucking listening to you. Go to hell or I'll fucking kill you.' They thought I was serious, but it was only a figure of speech. All my anger and my mental illness. I am not using my mental illness as an excuse, but that's just the way my mind worked, my adrenaline.

There is nothing linear about women's varied experiences with confinement in state and locally run agencies and past abuse, addiction, and mental illness. Maggie is quoted at some length here as she described her history of cycling in and out of formal control systems:

First off, I was in a mental hospital for three months ... [I] was hearing voices saying burn that unit down and you will die. They will evacuate everyone else, and you stay in your room, and they will think that you are gone, and you will die in the fire while they're gone. They extinguished the fire and they found me in the room after. That was my first crime as an adult ... After that, about a year and a half later I was feeling sick again. I was in the midst of [an abusive relationship]. I got married to a really wrong man, and I was after having a child. I was having problems with post-natal depression and psychotic depression. Then I married a man after I lost my child to adoption. I married a man who was physically and mentally abusive. And the other way, too [sexually abusive]. And so we separated after he beat me. He was after beating me that day. So I went to the Waterford and asked them for admission, and they wouldn't admit me. I had nowhere to go, so you have to do what you have to do. So I went down to the phone by the Waterford hospital and I called them and told them I had a gun but really it was only a plastic toy thing. I was crying out for help. It was a little plastic thing you get in a surprise package type of thing. And I told them I had a gun. I was trying to do it so they would shoot me to kill me. To give them a reason to shoot and kill me because I didn't want to live. I was basically trying to show the [system] that I was sick.

Countless other stories are related to young girls' entanglement with foster care providers and their subsequent criminalization. Leanne described her 'custody-care' continuum:

I've been seeing a psychiatrist and a psychologist since I was sixteen. That was all through my experience in foster care. I was in foster care when I was fifteen and sixteen. My mother and I didn't get along. That was how I first started getting in trouble because I was always running away from home.

Rachael also recounted her sense of hopelessness and despair of having her daughter taken from her because of her own childhood involvement with state care.

My second crime [as an adult] when I went federal was because I lost my daughter [to Child Welfare] and I just had enough of it. They said I couldn't take care of her because of my past. I was dealing with a lot at the time. My family, my friends, and overall my daughter being taken I just couldn't deal with it. I couldn't take it anymore. I lashed out. I purposely wanted to get caught.

The layers of social control experienced by many of these women as children and young girls continue to be a major force in their lives. Attempts to 'go straight' are strongly influenced by the nature and extent of these control mechanisms and are further discussed when the focus moves to reintegration.

Defiance of Gender Norms

Gender norms are a powerful societal tool for ensuring conformity (Andersen 2003). These informal processes of routine social interaction through which women are personally discredited or 'put in their place' often result in labelling women deviant (Schur 1984). Women's deviance, then, is a social construct that results from a particular kind of definition and response. As Howard Becker has argued, 'social groups create deviance by making the rules whose infraction constitutes deviance, and by applying these rules to particular people and labeling them as outsiders. From this point of view, deviance is not a quality of the act the person commits, but rather a consequence of the application by others of rules and sanctions to an 'offender' (1963: 9). Becker goes on to note that labels are applied unequally and are largely a matter of some persons or groups (in this case men) imposing their rules on others (women) (ibid.: 17). Deviant designations are assigned by those who hold the political and economic power. Women who 'offend' specific gender norms by behaving in ways deemed inappropriate for females receive the label 'deviant.' Beauty norms are one such example of the antisocial control (Carlen 2002) that is exerted over young girls and the associated pressures to have them conform to gender norms. Beauty norms govern the visual objectification of women and, as Schur makes clear, 'physical appearance is much more central to evaluations of women than it is to evaluations of men; this emphasis implicitly devalues women's other qualities and accomplishments; women's "looks" thereby become a commodity and a key determinant of 'success' or "failure"; the beauty norms used in evaluating women are excessively narrow and quite unrealistic; cultural reinforcement of such norms conveys to the ordinary woman a sense of perpetual "deficiency"' (1984: 68). Failing to satisfy the stringent requirements associated with physical appearances leads to a dual designation of deviance. Violation of beauty norms results in a deviant label in and of itself. Attempting to renegotiate these gendered boundaries leads to secondary deviance. Women often seek out other ways to assert themselves in contestation of these informal norms and, in doing so, are 'doubly deviant.' Several examples of women in defiance of beauty norms are cited in the interviews for this study. In Corrina's case, her attempts to resist the boundaries associated with physical appearances led her to sexual promiscuity and a further violation of sexuality norms. She explained:

> I never considered myself very pretty. Now I look at myself and if someone don't like me they don't have to look at me. But back then I was a teenager, and I wanted to be like everybody else. Small and pretty. So what I could do to fit in I done. That was my humour. And doing whatever, bend over backwards, doing whatever anybody wanted me to do. That included being taken advantage of by all the guys [for sexual purposes].

Other women have employed resistance strategies to the informal gender norms by turning to 'formally sanctioned deviance.' That is, to permeate the trappings of gender role expectations, they turn to illegal activities. Rachael, for example, who admittedly did not conform to prescribed beauty norms, took steps to compensate for her 'deficiency' and sought alternative means of gaining acceptance. This translated into becoming a runner for her peers, which included the ongoing provision of stolen goods. 'All my life I was told I was ugly. That I would never get anywhere. That I would never amount to anything. So I took it in my head that I would have to do things a bit different. Do what I had to do to get accepted. And that's just how it went.'

Kathleen described her non-conformity to female appearance norms as specific to a certain class and urban setting. She described her situation moving from a small rural town to a metropolitan centre where she did not fit in. A turn to criminal activity was her way of gaining the acceptance of her peers, negotiated through the acquisition of material signs of conformity:

> It was wicked. It's like you are different. You move into a place where you didn't grow up. And then to come in and move into [public] housing right off the bat you're an outcast. So you are going to do whatever you can to fit in, and I did. I done everything in my power. I fit in all right ... That's when I started shoplifting. I would go down to the mall and steal what I needed

... After that, I got kicked out of school. I got pregnant. I done everything ...
Yeah, I fit in. I made myself fit in. I was fitting in one way or another.

Another powerful tool for ensuring gender norm conformity is the notion of women as passive and nurturing. A masculine character structure requires self-confidence, independence, boldness, responsibility, risk-taking, and aggression and/or violence (Messerschmidt 1986: 40). Such characteristics are shunned for women, and transgressing these boundaries results in a deviant designation. Several women spoke about the consequences of violating this norm. For Katharine, her aggression and 'tomboyish' ways led to her being ostracized by her family:

> I was basically on the other end of any abuse. I was the aggressive person. Men, I didn't bother with them. Boyfriends came and went at that point. I was one of the guys. I was out beating around, We had our fun and I was out beating around and I had a really bad temper. And growing up in [Mundy Pond] there was a lot of people to meet. I was just out having fun like the guys but because I wasn't a guy, I drew a lot of attention. The wrong kind of attention.

Non-conformity to heterosexual relationships is another form of anti-social control for women who fail to satisfy gender norms. Speaking to the objectification of women, MacKinnon has asserted that 'sexuality is the linchpin of gender inequality' and further argued that '[a] woman is a being who identifies and is identified as one whose sexuality exists for someone else, who is socially male. Women's sexuality is the capacity to arouse desire in that someone (1982: 533).

Sexuality, then, becomes a major site of exclusion and isolation for lesbians who violate heterosexual norms. In my study, lesbians told of having to compensate in many ways for their denouncing heterosexuality, and therefore they sought out other forms of social approval. Oftentimes, this took the form of turning to drugs or alcohol to resist their sexuality-based exclusion from society.

Another of the pivotal regulators of women's conformity is the set of maternity norms (Welch 1997; Schur 1984). Maternity norms govern what is often viewed as women's primary traditional role – mothering. Despite changing family patterns and society's claim that it has loosened the traditional family construct, women are still expected not only to bear children but also to do so within the approved context of conventional marriage. As Schur has pointed out, 'the very terms used for childbearing outside of marriage – "unwed" or "unmarried" motherhood, and also "illegitimacy" itself – indicate both the character of the norm-violation and the strong social disapproval attaching to it' (1984: 83). Defying parenting norms is strictly a motherhood offence. Jessica spoke directly to her resistance of maternity norms when she had her first child as a single teenage mother: 'It all started when I got seventeen. It was like my life was over kind of thing [because I just had a child] and now I was supposed to go a certain way that I didn't want to go ... I was expected to stay home and look after a youngster. So, I just didn't care.' April talked about her rebellion against maternity norms and chronicles her 'breaking out' period:

> I wasn't a hard kid growing up ... I mean I was only young when I got pregnant and I more or less said, fuck, like my life is gone now anyways. So, just do what we can. I was young. I was free. Even though I had a child I didn't want to be tied down. So I just continued to live a teenage life and I got twisted.

Women's trajectories into prison are marked by often long-standing patterns of poverty, abuse, drug addictions, histories of formal social controls, and defiance of gender role norms. These factors converge in ways that are clearly non-linear. That is, these axes of exclusion frequently overlap to produce a lifestyle of often-unwanted dependencies on the state. In turn, these dependencies become further entrenched in a criminal justice system that fosters a culture of dependency and does nothing to contribute to women's economic and social empowerment. The compounding effects of incarceration on the lives of those women excluded by society based on class, gender, sexuality, and cultural differences form the focus of the next chapter, which moves us closer to deconstructing the notion of reintegration.

5 Doing Time on the Inside: Prisoning of Women

It's the system that's crazy, not the women.

Charmaine

Logically, localized criminal justice initiatives cannot be looked at without also examining prisons. The prison experience plays a major role in how women adjust (or not) to their period of localized release. How women experience and cope with the pains of imprisonment (Sykes 1958; Johnson and Toch 1982) affects their ability to reconcile the pains of release. The former are well documented to have long-lasting effects on the physical, psychological, economic, and social well-being of prisoners (McGee 2000; Martel 1999) and cannot be ignored in looking at women's experiences of reintegration. Indeed, women place a huge premium on their prison experiences as directly related to their reintegration efforts. Alternatively, certain characteristics of prison life are identified as having assisted their staying out of prison, for example, rehabilitative programming, employment counselling, substance abuse counselling, structured living environment, and peer supports. This chapter devotes considerable attention to women's experiences of incarceration and their carryover effects back in the outside world. From here, focus shifts to local factors that converge to either facilitate or block women's reintegration. While we know that the majority of women prisoners will return to their neighbourhoods at some point, we know very little about the reasons for women's so-called successes after prison, especially given the plethora of social, economic, political, and cultural inequalities that contribute to their criminalization.

Two-Tiered Prisons

As mentioned earlier, the Canadian penal system operates on two distinct levels.[1] The majority of women in this study had 'done time' in both provincial and federal institutions. A major emergent theme is the imbalance that exists between the two systems. Discussions of a two-tiered penal system feature prominently in relation to successes or failures post-prison. A second theme surfaced around the distinctions between the 'treatment' of criminalized males and females. A formal equality framework making men the comparator group upon which penal programs are based is not lost on women, despite the rhetoric of woman-centredness. Both themes are discussed in turn.

In Canada, women sentenced to terms of imprisonment of two years or more serve their sentences in federal prisons, by virtue of section 743(1) of the Criminal Code; sentences under two years result in a provincial prison term. In some instances, a woman may be permitted to serve a federal sentence in a provincial prison, under the Exchange of Services Agreement. There are a number of reasons why a woman would choose to remain in her home province, most notably to be closer to her family and children. Apart from geographical considerations, a most disturbing trend has been emerging in justice systems across the country. That is, women appearing in court are requesting federal sentences to avail themselves of the wider range of programming and treatment services offered in the federal system (Sweet 2003). This trend is startling against the backdrop of earlier discussions chronicling systemic human rights' violations of women federal prisoners in Canada (Canadian Human Rights Commission 2003). Nevertheless, this trend is echoed throughout my interviews by women who noted the discriminatory workings of the two-tiered penal system in Canada. Jennifer described her judicial plea to 'go federal':

> When I went to my last charge I asked the judge for over two years and he gave it to me. I felt in my own heart that the justice system in Newfoundland wasn't doing anything for me. Wasn't offering me the help I needed or the programs I need to get me back on my feet. In a way I was kind of saying to him, 'Like what is the sense of putting me back in Clarenville and staying there a while and getting out and not handling it and then going back again?' Like if I was getting counselling or programs or some-

thing like that then maybe I would be able to stay out. But there is none of that here in Newfoundland. Not for women anyways.

Corrina discussed the so-called merits of the federal system and related an incident at the provincial prison that led her to request a federal transfer partway through her sentence so that she could continue her studies:

> If I went, if I was foolish enough to do something and the judge looked at me and gave me under two years I'd have to punch someone out in the courtroom to try and get over two years. I would never be able to go to Clarenville again. Never. Like I was going to school in Clarenville taking a carpentry course from CONA [College of the North Atlantic] and I was studying for a really, really big test one night and one of the girls she put the place up. It was a sin because she was on all kinds of medication. But the more she screamed the more they bugged her. So I was up all night. I went in to do the test and I forgot everything. I lost it right in the middle of the school room. I flipped out. Having anxiety attacks. They had to give me Ativan. After that I got transferred federal.

Rachael commented on the reality that many women prisoners lack family supports on the outside and how this effectively excludes any desire they might otherwise have to remain in a provincial prison based on its proximity to their places of origin:

> When I went to court I was only getting I think twelve months and I asked for twenty-four months ... Like I had no visitors. If I had done a provincial term I would not have had any money, no tobacco, none of my family was in support of coming for visitation so there was no reason for me to stay in town and that is why I wanted to go away.

Jennifer has been in and out of provincial and/or federal prisons and psychiatric hospitals for almost twenty years. She talked about recent regressive changes that have taken place at the Newfoundland and Labrador Correctional Centre for Women (NLCCW) which propelled her request for a federal term:

> When I assaulted that police officer they told me I might get a year, and I approached my family and I never done that before. I said I am going to ask to go two years or more. That's when my brother said you have to start

talking about why you don't want to go back to Clarenville because you practically grew up there. I knew I wasn't going to get the help I needed in Clarenville. I spent more time in the chair, the restraint chair, than I did out with the other inmates. I beat up three guards there in one morning who were trying to restrain me.

Rebecca focused on the benefits of getting 'fast-tracked' through the federal system and how this serves as an incentive for women to request federal time:

Women are asking judges for federal time. Well that's what my sister did. Her lawyer asked for federal. It was the only way she could get programs. She could work and get money to support herself up there. And she was automatically fast-tracked. If you get a federal sentence and you stay in provincial prison you lose all your federal rights. You don't get fast-tracked and you lose a lot of other things. Stupid.

For women like Nicole, who want to be able to participate in addictions programs upon release, the programs in localities surrounding federal prisons are an important feature that would be unavailable to them through a provincial prison sentence:

When I was on parole they [parole officers] didn't want to help me go to school. They couldn't even give me a bus pass or nothing. You are just there. I mean I asked them about programs and stuff but there was nothing [in the community]. Now when I was in Nova Scotia, Halifax, on parole for one month I did programs in Antigonish. Thirty-one day programs for addictions. I broke my glasses in jail and I told my parole officer about it, and he picked them up right way and got them fixed. Down here they don't do any of that.

The opportunity to earn some income while federally incarcerated is a very real issue for women like Nicole who do not have financial supports on the outside to help carry them through their prison sentences.

They [federal and provincial systems] are both completely different. If you are in federal prison your time is taken up. You are doing stuff. They pay you for it, too, right? You get your canteen every two weeks because you are working. If you are in provincial and you don't have family you don't get nothing, right?

Programming availability, however limited, is often cited as a major reason for wanting to 'go federal.' Nicole highlighted the range of programming that she participated in while in a federal prison:

> I did a lot of anger management and Survivors of Sexual Abuse and Trauma in Truro. I went to school there, did upgrading. I did horticulture up there. I did some AA. There are a lot of things you can do up there. It is all provided for you. You didn't have to go anywhere. I did find them helpful, especially the SLE [Structured Living Environment] program up in Nova. You are living there and they give you [all kinds of help].

The situation at the NLCCW, in terms of limited space and lack of mental health services, poses major problems for women. Laura explained:

> Were you ever there [in Clarenville]? Do you know how small it is? It takes your life away. That's what it does. I was taking pills. Trying to cope. You weren't allowed to do anything unless they said. It's just too hard. It's too small. I couldn't have stayed in Clarenville to serve my federal time. I would have cracked up with that little bit of space. So I made my choice to go federal.

A lack of provincial mental health services is also a catalyst for requesting federal time:

> One day one of the girls, she was handicapped, and another girl said something to her about shaving her legs and I lost it! I flipped. I walked out into the office and said if I don't get transferred today I am going to kill someone. Everyone is here trying to do their time, and the ones here with mental health problems gets fucking picked on. I said it's disgusting. I want out of here.

Many women talked about getting in a federal prison the much sought after help they needed and wanted to deal with their issues, help that is unavailable to them through other non-penal agencies. Yvonne talked about first starting to come to terms with her abusive past while in a federal prison:

> I did federal time. Two years plus a day in Kingston. I got a lot of help up there, too. That helped me benefit the most. Dealing with all my abuse and

stuff started up there. That's where it started. Like I had a lot of behavioural problems through anger. I still carries that but I am getting a lot better. I am getting help that was not there at first. When I went federal time I finally started to get some help.

A two-tiered penal system is evidenced in terms of the gendered availability of services, programs, and physical space for female and male prisoners. Rebecca commented at some length in describing these gendered prison conditions.

There's a lot of difference between men and women. For instance, if you are out in Clarenville and you are cursing on someone you are locked down. Down at HMP [Her Majesty's Penitentiary][2] they wouldn't do that. The Pen[itentiary] has more. You can get paid at HMP ... The men [guards] out there is a fucking pain, too. That should never, never, never be. They should never put a male guard in a women's prison. They can roam up and down those halls, and you could be in the bathroom. The men have a lot more programs. There is not a thing in this town for women. Everything is for men. There is no focus on employment and education. You can't even get a TA [temporary absence] to do anything. There is nothing out there to do anything else. It's just somewhere to shove you. They got nothing out there just one big empty room. They took it all away from the women and gave it to the men and the women got the shaft. And the men had the nerve to complain because at the lock-up we had a fucking TV. Wow. Try looking at what you got compared to what we got.

For Rebecca, the revolving door of the provincial prison is exacerbated by the lack of supports in place for women to handle the underlying issues that brought them into prison and that coexist to keep them coming back:

Out there [NLCCW] it's just one big fucking empty space. You are in the woods almost. You are right off the road. There is nothing. At least men down at the pen, if there are outside AA meetings they could go to them. Anger management is outside the building and they go. They can at least go out and do a bit of work out around.

Clearly, there is a major shortage of programs in women's prisons. Such programs as are available for women, for example, peer support and substance abuse programs, albeit in extremely limited supply, are available in federal prisons only.

Criminalizing Mental Illness

In Canada, prisons have now become the last resort for dealing with the mentally ill. Prisons are the only places that cannot turn women (and men) away from their doors. The criminal justice system continues to be the net used to catch all those unfortunate individuals who fall through the ever-widening gaps in our health care system. As a result, women with mental illnesses, which all too often are brought about or exacerbated by the debilitating effects of institutional life, are trapped in a systemic spiral of so-called help networks that are neither designed to deal with them nor accommodate their needs.

The criminalization of mental illness is marked by a number of key elements, as outlined by Kaiser (2004). These include: an overrepresentation of people with mental health problems in the criminal justice system; dissonance between the purposes and services of the justice system compared with the needs of mentally ill detainees; exacerbation of symptomology and diminution of social function as a result of the ineptitude and insensitivity of the criminal justice system; heightened likelihood of recidivism because of the combined problems of an underfunded mental health care system and an unresponsive justice system. The Canadian Mental Health Association (CMHA) provides an understanding of this social phenomenon: 'The mentally ill are being jailed rather than helped due to the lack of community mental health services ... The trigger for police involvement is usually a nuisance offence, but the mentally ill are spending more and more time in police custody because local mental health services are insufficient and those that exist are over-burdened. In fact, once mentally ill persons are involved with the police, there is a 81% chance they will be apprehended again within a two-year period because they still have not accessed adequate services' (cited in Kaiser 2004: 7). Prisons, which have punishment and security, as their primary goals, are ill-equipped to provide psychiatric care and treatment to mentally ill persons. Prisons are not mental health treatment centres and they should not claim to be. However, an increasing number of individuals with psychiatric diagnoses are ending up behind bars.

Lurigio has examined the mental health service needs of individuals within the penal system and identified three major policy shifts contrib-

uting to the criminalization of mental illness: first came the deinstitutionalization of mental health patients from psychiatric hospitals into
locally based centres; this policy, however, was never properly implemented and failed to provide adequate or well-coordinated outpatient
care: 'in other words, the unsuccessful transition to community mental
health care had the most tragic effects on patients least able to handle
the basic tasks of daily life' (2001: 447). Second came mental health law
reforms that have placed restrictions on the procedures and criteria for
involuntary commitment; therefore, only the 'most dangerous and profoundly mentally ill are hospitalized, resulting in greatly increased
numbers of mentally ill persons in the community who may commit
criminal acts and enter the criminal justice system' (ibid.: 448). Third
came the compartmentalization of mental health and other treatment
services, which has the result that patients with 'dual diagnoses' are
being refused acceptance into one or both programs or centres.

Based on these policy shifts, an alarming trend has been developing
in Canada in recent decades – the number of women entering the
prison system with diagnoses of mental illness has been increasing at a
disturbing rate (Peters 2003). Leanne commented on this pattern:

> There are a lot of women in jails who are depressed or got anxiety and
> didn't even know it. There is not enough talk about it with doctors or any-
> one to say what is on your mind. [The] psychiatrist, he is only in once a
> month. If you do get to see him it's for about ten minutes and that's it.

The lack of appropriate treatment programs and personnel to attend
to the unique needs of mentally ill detainees is a major source of frustration, not only for such detainees but for other prisoners, who feel
that these women should either not be imprisoned in the first place or
should at least have special provisions during their stays. Sarah talked
about the volatility of having prisoners with mental illness mixed in
with the general population.

> There should be a separate place for mental health. They are saying they
> are fit to stand trial. I've seen it where they would smack someone right in
> the head with the broom. Walking around, big smiles on their face, don't
> talk very much but then pick up a TV and smash it against the floor and
> then go after people for no reason. Down in the dining room eating and
> there's cups flying and you're ducking and they are splitting their fucking
> heads open. And then they are putting them in segregation for months.

And why? That person has got a mental problem. They don't know they are doing these things or why they are doing it. They are thinking probably you are trying to do something to hurt them. They should not be there. They [guards] have not got the training.

Sarah, too, talked about the inhumanity of confining women with severe mental health problems in a prison:

I seen a girl in there for the same length of time as me, six months, and out of six months she spent five and a half in her room and the rest of it crying and singing out and saying her prayers saying, 'Please help me. God help me. These people, I don't know what they are doing to me.' Then she starts crying and everyone has to get out of the dining room because this person is yelling out and screaming. Then there are people who are suicidal, blankets up over them. You can't let them out of your sight for a second. These kind of people should be in a [separate] place. They should have, like they got down to the men's prison, where all MHAs[3] are in one section doing their time together, PCs [Protective Custody] are doing their time.

Jennifer also elucidated the differential treatment of women prisoners with psychiatric problems:

If I even got a little upset I was put in what they call the hole or segregation. And so I spent most of my time there isolated from everyone else. That's the way it has been for me 90 per cent of my life. I try and do something that is going to make me better but something always gets in the way. But like I was only eleven when I had my first suicide attempt so I've been in the psychiatric system ever since. Either way it goes.

Corrina discussed the treatment available to mentally ill prisoners and the deleterious effects of incarceration on one's psychological well-being:

I used to see a psychiatrist on a regular basis. When I transferred to Nova I was on fourteen different kinds of pills. Antidepressants. All different kinds. I've heard it said that the highest rate of people taking medication in Nova comes from Newfoundland. There are more people with mental health problems in Clarenville than there are people just out doing normal crime. They haven't got the space. The guards are not equipped to handle it. What are they going to do? Strip them down, hog-tie them to a chair and male guards at that helping? It's gross. These people don't need it. There is an imbalance somewhere in the brain. Why do they have to put up with that? I've seen them put [name of mentally ill inmate] in that [restraint] chair for hours and hours tied down to that chair, in the hallway by her room door. They wonder why she is up screaming all night. They had her hog-tied to a chair for God's sake! Make no wonder she is the way she is.

Charmaine brought into focus the unique needs of this population of women, many of whom cycle back and forth from prisons to psychiatric hospitals and have never known life outside an institution:

[It's the system] that is crazy, not the women. In Clarenville, you are all put together in one little room. You do everything in that room. Make no wonder there is always fights and people always flipping out. MHAs put in with the regular population. I am not saying they are any different but they have greater needs. They should not be there.

Valerie provided a chilling example of the abuses that take place inside institutions and the reality that prison can sometimes represent a safer place than a mental hospital:

I never had nowhere to go [when I got out of prison]. I used to take overdoses just to get in the hospital. I sued the Health Care a few years ago too. I was sexually assaulted while I was in hospital. It was hard and very scary being paranoid and all that shit. I don't think I was ever dependent on prison [unclear]. I think the hospital had more control over me than the prison.

Disturbing comparisons are drawn between the treatment that women receive in psychiatric hospitals and the prison system – placement in the latter is often the preferred 'choice.' Yvonne compared the treatment she received in both institutions:

Honestly, I was treated better in Clarenville than I was treated in the Health Care system. They didn't lock me down. In the Waterford I was locked down for three months in a hole. Shit and piss on the floor and live in it. Shock treatments. No chance, needles. Slap your food down. Wouldn't let you use the washroom. They treated me good out there [prison] compared to the hospitals. I've got to be honest. In the Waterford I didn't eat for forty days and forty nights.

A high degree of incongruency between the institution-based psychiatric diagnoses that women received and their self-reports is also a source of ongoing concern. Valerie explained:

> I have been off medication now two years. I was told all my life that I was bipolar. [Doctor] even said that I am going to need my medication again. That I am going to fall. Two years now have passed and I am better than I ever was on medication. I haven't been at the Waterford for years. I hate to go in there. As soon as I walk in I get ill. I see [my psychiatrist] at his office.

Institutional responses all too often result in overdiagnosing and overmedicating women. Jennifer related her experiences in this regard:

> [Psychiatrist] still don't believe that I had a very serious drug problem. He said I was bipolar. I think it's starting to sink in now that I did have a drug problem. I remember at the Waterford and patients wouldn't take their pills. I would line up and take their pills for God's sake. Or they'd slip it under their tongue and give it to me. I didn't mind being out of it.

Valerie has been out of the prison system now for almost three years. She talked about coping with past abuse without using the prescription medications that she had been given in the psychiatric hospital and then through the prison system:

> The only problem I had going off my medication is that now I had feelings. It was hard for us [she and her partner] for a while because I couldn't communicate right. Medication always blocks it out. That's what everybody believes. Everyone thinks if you take your medication all your problems are gone. Same as taking drugs. To numb out the pain. Same as slashing. It's gone for a few minutes and then it's back. I do believe that getting out of the system is a big part of it [recovery]. I was totally institutionalized.

For some women, like Leanne, initial psychiatric diagnoses were made at an early age when they were resident at various state custodial agencies:

> I used to always get heart palpitations. Look at my hands. Sweaty, clammy. Nervousness. A lot of it is social anxiety. When I am around a lot of people it feels like a panic attack. It must be like, I am diagnosed with a depression but I don't feel depressed. When I was seventeen they diag-

nosed me with that. When I was in Whitbourne, that's when they put me on drugs. Paxil.

For others, like Jamie, the cycle of depression began as a result of dealing with the pains of abuse: 'It all started [depression] about twenty-one or twenty-two. I got married because I was pregnant and it was the wrong thing to do. I just got sicker and sicker and sicker. I was into an abusive marriage that I didn't want to be into.'

Several women spoke about resisting the administration of prescription medications that prison psychiatrists offered to them. Rebecca explained her rationale for doing so:

> They [prison psychiatrists] offered me pills. They said I was overly compulsive. Overly compulsive got nothing to do with it. They wanted to put me on meds. That would make more problems for me. Sure you are only getting rid of the problem for a little while. Medicate you and keep you quiet while you are inside.

For many women, mental illness is self-reportedly situational. That is, there is a tendency to psychologize women's resistant behaviour inside the prison. Jamie explained:

> A lot of people get addictions once they get inside. There was a young girl out there and I am telling you we could not eat with the woman. The food was dribbling down her face. She couldn't keep her eyes open she was pilled up that much. I met her three years ago. She got a baby as bright as can be. All they done was medicate her to shut her up. Give her a few pills and you won't have to deal with her. That is their way of dealing with things. To up her medication because she is flipping out. Instead of finding out why. That girl came out and I am telling you she is just like a normal girl walking down the road. And I thought there was something seriously wrong with her when we were locked up.

Rebecca talked about depression and other psychiatric diagnoses brought about by the very conditions of imprisonment:

> It's normal to be depressed when you're locked up. That's normal. So why give you depression pills? They tell me I should be on depression pills. I don't want it. I haven't got no chemical imbalance. I am depressed, yeah. Let me go back to school and I wouldn't be depressed. Put me in school

and you would see a different person here. Instead of saying is there something we can do to get you out of trouble they drug you up.

For some women, like Leanne, the diagnosis of a mental illness is only made once they have entered into the prison system:

[Recently] the doctor diagnosed me with an anxiety. I was having panic attacks. So he gave me antidepressant, anxiety pills. I forget what they were called. I found that I did need that because since I started taking it I see a difference in myself. I was always kept to myself and felt like the walls were caving in and stuff. I think that was a big part of why I was drinking and taking drugs so I didn't have to feel that way anymore. Now that I am medicated for it and I am feeling better I got to continue taking that when I am out.

Despite earlier discussions favouring the wider availability of programming and psychiatric services at federal prisons, there is no shortage of commentary that is highly critical of the lack of appropriate, gender-based programming at both levels. Again, even though the quantity and quality of programming at federal prisons is somewhat of an enticement for women wishing to avail themselves of support services, this is a 'lesser of two evils' rationale. Appropriate support services are lacking at both the federal and the provincial levels. Sarah commented on this situation:

They haven't got anything for women [in prison]. Well, they've got an old nun that's out there [NLCCW] and she don't know the first thing about it. How would she know about anger management? Like if I were really, really pissed off, if I was angry and I said I am going to tear someone's head off. I am going to go out there and I am literally going to bang them to the wall and I am literally going to kill them on the floor or something. So they are probably going to take me and put me some place up there with the lifers. You are saying it out of the blue because you are mad.

Jennifer raised the issue of long waiting lists for psychiatric services in prison and the lack of appropriate responses to deal with mentally ill prisoners:

In Clarenville if you get really agitated they take you to the hospital and get a shot and then bring you back and put you in the restraint chair until you fall asleep. In Springhill there is always a doctor there ... The justice system is so different all across Canada. I was there for thirteen months at one point and I never so much as seen the psychiatrist. Half the time you would go four or five months without seeing any doctor.

For women like Charmaine, who has been going back and forth to prison for almost two decades for shoplifting charges, programs geared specifically to her offences are lacking:

They don't have it [Stoplifters[4]] here in St John's and they should. For the women or the men, too, there is a lot of men shoplifters but most of these men do have alcohol or drugs problems, and I'm not condemning them, and there is a lot of women out there with alcohol and drug problems who shoplift, too, that contribute to their habit. But there is a lot of women out there, too, who shoplift because it's an addiction. They probably started out for survival but it ended up as an addiction. Like me, all the times that I went to jail I got nothing out of it. I got no programs, I got nothing. Sit down and eat, smoke, drink Pepsi all day long. That's all we done.

Finally, Rebecca related the need for more meaningful programs for women to assist them upon their release:

There needs to be programming here [for women] because there is none. They [women] need more counselling groups in here. Like group sessions. One-on-one groups and some way to continue those groups when you get out. And probably an employment counsellor who can look at your goals and work out a plan for when you get out. If you are not getting the help you need from alcohol and drugs you got no other choice but to go out and commit crimes to feed your habit. You got no other choice. You are going to end up back in here anyways.

Institutionalizing Women

For many criminalized women, patterns of institutionalization begin long before their initial entry into the prison system. Prison represents just one more journey in and out of state-sponsored institutions including psychiatric hospitals and foster care. Women's institutional experiences and dependencies are inextricably tied into their attempts to negotiate their independence upon release. Institutionalization stands as an important marker between those women who 'make it' upon their release and those who continue to be drawn back into one control system or another. Valerie has been in institutions for more than thirty years; she described this vicious cycle of retrenched dependency on state-imposed norms and regulations:

I have been institutionalized since I was eleven. That's all I have ever known. I've never known what it's like to be out living like a normal life. I was always hurting myself. I never ever hurt anyone in my life. I always cut myself up or overdosed. I even apologized to the judge that day. When I went to Clarenville I had to see a priest. I had to. I never ever hurt no one. It was the first time I ever hurt anyone and I was so drugged up.

For someone like Jennifer, normal functioning and expressions of one's feelings, whether negative or positive, are met only with punishment in an institutional setting:

I have been institutionalized for the past twenty-five years. I never even had the opportunity to say I was feeling a bit down and I was carted off in a cop car somewhere. Plus the school didn't help me very much. I ran away and things like that. I was ten years old and I'd be gone for days just sitting in the country in the woods smoking cigarettes.

Sadly, for many women like Nicole, institutional life offers a degree of familiarity and comfort that they have never known on the outside:

After so long I kind of got used to the system and it seemed like it was starting to [feel like home]. Being out here [in the community] it is kind of hard. When you are walking around you can still see the bars and stuff. You can still see the Seg and the steel doors and [hear the guards] and stuff. It is hard to get away from it. Out here it seems like nobody in the world [cares]. I don't know how to verbalize it. I just feel it. I don't know how to talk to anybody cause in there at least out there [in prison] your life is laid out for you. I have looked for a place out here but right now I am thinking about going back to Nova again. At least that was my home. There I have everything. There's nothing out here. If you got a criminal record nobody is going to hire you. I don't have the training. There is no housing and stuff. If you don't want to go back and you want to stay clean it's almost impossible. I just wish I was back [in Truro]. There is nobody out here to talk to. Everyday is a struggle.

Leanne, who has now been out of institutions (prisons and psychiatric hospitals) for the longest period in her adult life expressed her feelings of frustration and isolation on the outside:

> I got nothing right now. I am looking for a place at the moment. I have
> been here [in a halfway house] six months. I just want to go back at Nova.
> Out here you need a damage deposit, you need housing, a place that is
> warm, a place to call your own. Out here it is impossible. You can't do it. I
> can't do it by myself.

Similarly, for Jamie, life in prison effectively removes the loneliness that
she experiences on the outside. She weighed the benefits and shortcomings of doing time in the prison versus being in her own home: 'I don't
know if it is a safe place [in prison] but there's lots of company. Lots of
different people to talk to. At home, there is no one to talk to. It is
lonely.'

Maggie, who has been out of the prison system for three years, recognized the detrimental effects of locking someone away in an institution
and the debilitating consequences of this isolation:

> If they had to keep me in the prison system past three years and I had to
> keep on with the hard crowds and learning all the prison terminologies
> and then put me out on the streets ten years later, to be honest with you, I
> probably could kill somebody. With all the anger I would have built up
> inside. I am angry now. But if I had to let that anger build up, if my mother
> had to die or my father had to die while I was inside and when I came out
> I would have went looking for that judge and I would have spit in his
> fucking face.

A hierarchy of institutional so-called preferences is a key theme. Quite
disturbingly, prison often represents a place that feels safer than confinement in a psychiatric hospital. Nicole explained:

> I was going back and forth to the Waterford Hospital for years but I just
> couldn't handle it. It's just so cold in there. Like the nurses and the doctors,
> they are supposed to be there and be caring and stuff but I found it so cold.
> Don't seem like it is a hospital. I had so much abuse in there [hospital] I
> can't even begin to tell you. That's the last place I want to go.

Most disturbingly, time spent in psychiatric hospitals is often as trau-
matizing as prison, or even more so. Jennifer spoke of the abuses that
she encountered while in psychiatric 'care':

There have been times when I have got upset and they had to put me in what they calls their TQ room [Therapeutic Quiet]. It's just a room with a mattress. Same practically as that down at the lock-up. They [the Waterford staff] are like prison guards who can do a lot to you when they are not on camera. They can, and they don't hesitate.

Jamie, who has been out of prison for years, is now a regular inpatient at the Waterford Hospital. She talked about her life inside psychiatric institutions:

I have been to hell and back again, you could call it. Been to hell and back again. My life growing up in the hospitals was way worse than it is in jail. I mean in here [the hospital] there is no freedom. You can't go and come when you feel like it. That's the hardest part about being in here is depression and stuff. That's something else all together, that is. Their answer is to whack pills at you and [that] makes you very vulnerable.

The connection between prolonged involvement in state-controlled institutions and a woman's chances of making it one the outside were made clear in the following comment by Yvonne: 'I am totally institutionalized. I am only out a day or two and back again. I am back and forth to the Waterford for fourteen years. If that's not institutionalized I don't know what is. I have never lived a normal life. I don't know what that's like.' Nicole highlighted the lingering psychological effects of institutionalization that inhibit reintegration efforts on the outside:

After a while, you get so used to being inside that it becomes second nature to you. Your senses get all dulled out and you are afraid to make a decision on your own, afraid that you might get in trouble for making the wrong one. You go around in a daze most of the time and then you come out here and don't know which way is which. Prison is like my home. In there, everybody knows me and knows what I am all about and I know what they're all about. There's no big surprises.

Past abuses and other fears are associated with living alone on the outside for a person with a psychiatric illness, and Maggie summed up the sad reality of independent living for such individuals: 'It's hard to look at someone and tell them you feels safer in prison than you do outside. But that's the way it is for me.'

Much has been written on the painfulness of imprisonment for women (see, e.g., Morash and Schram 2002). The well-noted separation

from children and geographical isolation are undoubtedly very trau-
matic. Although the women in my sample did reiterate these concerns,
their pain was more often expressed in terms of their physical and emotional treatment within the prison system. Maggie shared her memory
of a singular incident, while at the same time noting that such inhumane practices are commonplace:

> You know what broke my heart one time in Springhill? There was this doc-
> tor nurse and he bought me a teddy bear. Someone to hug and he made me
> feel safe. One time I acted up and they put me in segregation and they took
> it on me. They told me if I didn't quieten down they were going to rip the
> ears off it. You know what they did? They opened the window and they
> ripped him up and they stuffed him on me. I have nightmares about that.
> I even had a name on him. It was 'Little Positive Buddy.' They must have
> thought there was something wrong in Springhill to give a teddy bear to a
> grown woman.

Several women commented on the recent introduction by provincial
prison authorities of a so-called restraint chair, which Jennifer described
to me:

> It's like an electrocution chair. They used to put a hockey helmet on my
> head. And they would put me in the chair and there would be a guard
> there just staring at me until I fell asleep ... [T]hey would make arrange-
> ments for the cops to come and take me to the hospital and then get an
> injection, bring me back in the chair until I fell asleep. Then the same thing
> would happen over and over again.

Sarah commented on the mental anguish of being separated from her
children and her inability to provide care for them while she was in
prison:

> The hardest thing about being out there doing your time is your children
> and who is looking after them and it goes through your head, you know,
> did he fall down and get hurt? Who is hugging him when he cries? I went
> through fucking hell and back and thinking about him and he was only
> seven years old and his father is drinking ... [I] came in and fourteen or six-
> teen days later the psychiatrist came in she said I heard you haven't been
> eating, you haven't been drinking, you haven't been getting any sleep. So
> she gave me some nerve pills. You are just constantly thinking about
> home, your kids.

Jennifer has severe mental health problems. She described a situation at federal prison that led her to launch a formal complaint against the prison staff:

> They [correctional staff] were notified that evening that I had planned on catching fire to myself and they never confronted me or made any attempts to talk to me or anything like that, and then when I did it, of course, they didn't take me to hospital. I was just left there in the cell for two days until the minister came in talking to me, and I showed her my sides and my arms, and she went out and made some calls, and next thing I knew I was taken to the hospital and flown to a burn unit and I had six surgeries, and then they came and told me I was being transferred to Saskatchewan.

Coping with prison life very often results in new-found dependencies on drugs, as Sarah explained:

> I'd say [substance abuse is] 98 per cent [of getting through prison]. Because when you go in there you can't cope with it unless you got something for your nerves to keep you calm. Then you can't sleep, you need a sleeping pill. So if you are there any length of time, by the time you come out you are addicted to the drugs. And then when you go back, they say you got a problem with drugs. Well, who put me on these drugs?

Similarly, Victoria traced her addictions to her initial prison sentence:

> I got into pills once I walked through those prison doors in 1995. I didn't know about taking pills, getting high. Swallowing pills to me [meant] taking an aspirin. [Then I got into] Demerol, Morphine, Valium, Percocet. Anything to give you a high even if it was a downer. Like Valium is a downer. It relaxed me. It took everything away from my mind. I was happy. I would take whatever I could get. I liked downers too. I guess it killed all the pain. I didn't have to deal with things. You didn't really care. You were relaxed and happy-go-lucky.

Jennifer described the psychological difficulties of trying to cope inside prison: 'The first time you say don't eat for a few days they say you are depressed and suicidal. You've heard of lock-downs and they can go on for days. Thinking about everything. Everything is going through your head. Sure that is enough to put anyone over the edge.'

It is quite clear from the above discussions that prisons do not empower women (Hannah-Moffat 2000; Pollack 2000). Quite the contrary. Isolation, deprivation, loss of liberty, infantilization, and medicalization are all features of the penal apparatus. Given the pathways into prison and the fundamental disempowerment of prisoners, how do women begin to rebuild once they are physically released from the pains of a prison existence? Getting out and trying to achieve some semblance of normalcy against the inhumanity and cruelty that characterize the prison is the focus of the next chapter.

6 Getting Out: Immediate and Measurable Transitions

For almost any woman, the relief of *getting* out of prison is quickly replaced by the anxiety of being out.

Faith (1993: 170, emphasis in original)

The transition from prison back into the outside world is a very difficult and anxious time for anyone. The challenges facing women upon release are compounded by systemic gendered inequalities in society. As Eaton has pointed out: 'Whatever disadvantages the woman suffered from before prison she now faces the world with the added disadvantage of a prison experience and a prison record. She is a prisoner and she brings this knowledge, this identity, out into the world. The prison experience will affect her response to the outside world, the prison record will affect the response of others to her. When she comes out, she brings something of the prison with her' (1993: 56).

All of the women in this study commented on the level of intimidation, disorientation, and trepidation that they felt about their release and the pressures of trying to resume their pre-prison identities. Yvonne described her fears in this regard:

> Believe me it was really hard coming out [of prison]. It was really scary. I wanted to go back in again. You can get institutionalized very easily, and what makes you institutionalized is the safety you feel inside. You know what I mean? I've been back and forth between prison and the Waterford for fifteen years. It's a scary world all around.

Nicole elaborated on the psychological adjustment of leaving the prison where attitudes of incompetence and low self-esteem are fostered:

It's like you're on the bus and you think it's written on your forehead that you just came out of prison. It's terrible, it is. You got no one around. It's much easier in prison because all the guards were around. They cared about you somewhat. Out here it just seems like you are by yourself. Just thrown out. And you are always being judged.

Taken-for-granted everyday tasks such as banking, shopping, or taking public transportation pose major stumbling blocks upon immediate release. Maggie described her initial encounter at the grocery store during her first few days out:

I went up there and I was frightened to death. I didn't know what to do and then I got into the wrong line-up. The woman told me I had too much stuff and I got panicked. I ended up telling her I just got out of prison. Then they wanted ID to change my welfare cheque and all I had was my parole card. I just left the cart and got out of there.

Safe and Affordable Housing

One of the immediate concerns facing women upon their release is the arduous process of securing safe and affordable housing (see, e.g., O'Brien 2001; Richie 2001). Much is dependent or getting settled in a place of one's own in order to qualify for welfare benefits, which require a fixed and permanent address. Reuniting with children is also contingent on the woman securing suitable accommodations. For most women living in poverty, finding an affordable place to live is difficult enough prior to any prison sentence, let alone afterwards, when there is the added burden of having to declare your recent residence to potential landlords.

For many women, the road out of prison often leads back to cohabitating in former relationships – relationships characterized by abuse. Corrina described her ordeal with inadequate housing arrangements and how this contributed to further abuse and isolation:

My daughter was [with me when I got out]. We were in a shelter for a while, and then I got a place with a girl I met in there [shelter] and we shared an apartment. Then, Christmas came and one of our friends punched me in the face. I had him charged. He is like 6'2" and a couple of hundred pounds ... That started the Percocet [painkillers] then. After that I went to a shelter for abused women in [southern Ontario] ... Then [lived] with a friend, then with a guy I met because I had nowhere else to go. I took a job at [a coffeeshop] to get enough money to leave to come home [to Newfoundland]. I got on the bus to come home, got stranded in Halifax, ran out of money there. I stayed at a shelter in Halifax. I didn't want to go to welfare because I would have had to change shelters ... [S]o after a while it was just easier to go back to the abuse.

Managing to secure decent accommodations can often mean the difference between staying out during that crucial first few months of release and going back inside. All too often, women end up in undesirable neighbourhoods characterized by poverty and violence, in accommodations which are wholly inadequate. Victoria described the burden of trying to find decent housing:

You don't have a lot of decent housing here. For some people that isn't an issue to go back but for some women it is. When I came here the carpet was filthy. I was stressed to the max. And you know something? You might not think it is a big thing but it was dirty. I don't like dirt. I was so stressed out. I was like I got to move. That stressed me out.

Slum housing becomes the all-too-familiar last resort for many women like Yvonne: 'Some of the places they put you in are not fit. That's what leads people back into jail. They are not fit at all. They shouldn't be allowed.'

In rural areas of the province of Newfoundland and Labrador the affordable housing crisis is even more pronounced. Emily described this ordeal and her attempt to alert policymakers to this problem:

I've been in touch with some politicians, and they told me there was no housing problems in rural communities in Newfoundland. In small communities houses are handed down from generation to generation. But what about the fact that there are children, now adults, living with parents or some relative because they don't have a house to go to? But saying you don't have a housing issue is saying you are willing to allow the abuse. You can call it silent abuse but the only reason it is silent is because everyone in the community is going to keep it quiet.

Leanne, a young unattached woman, noted the low housing priority given to single women: 'I just don't have the money to go and get my own place. Welfare is not going to give me my own place because I don't have any kids. I got to stay with somebody, and everyone I knows lives up around that area and the same friends I got, they got.'

Housing arrangements specific to Aboriginal women and their families are almost non-existent in this province, especially on the island. Nicole, an Inuit woman, noted the irony in this situation: 'I heard there was housing [at the Native Friendship Centre]. It's supposed to be for men and women, but they don't take anyone out of prison. Half of the people who are Native got a criminal record!'

Emmanuel House, a housing shelter in St John's that serves both men and women is often a stopover, temporary housing arrangement for a large number of women coming out of prison. Although many women prefer women-only accommodations (Eaton 1993), this is not an option. Emily described this situation: 'There's two beds here at [Emmanuel House] in all of St John's for [women] parolees. Compared to the number of Newfoundland and Labrador women in need that is not very good odds.'

Because Emmanuel House also houses men, arrangements specific to the needs of women more generally, and criminalized women specifically, are notably absent. Sarah remarked on this shortcoming:

> There should be some other kind of place in this city to house women who are not high risk, so their kids can come down, and they should have visits every evening after supper even for an hour in the evening and weekends. If they had a house like Emmanuel House and it had a lot of bedrooms for the women coming out, five rooms for little girls and boys and they could live in that place with their kids and a counsellor twenty-four-hours around the clock and those people had a home and that would be there.

For some women, securing any type of housing proved unsuccessful. Homelessness is the only remaining alternative. Jennifer recalled her time spent on the streets of St John's:

> I lived on the streets. One night the cops picked me up down on Quidi Vidi Lake, and I was unconscious in the gazebo. I was going back and forth there for months. It was so cold I guess I passed out from the cold. If you lose your apartment by going to jail you have to wait for thirty days to get another place.

Poverty is inextricably linked to the limited availability of housing alternatives for women. Rachael described the endless cycle that she is faced with:

> Poverty is the biggest factor because I mean when you come out [of prison] and you got no money. When I first got released I had nowhere to go. I had to stay in a hotel. I only had $300 to my name and I had to pay that in hotels. I had a bedsitting room first, and then that fell apart because I didn't have enough money to keep that going. That's the thing. If you're on social assistance, they don't give you a lot and you are shagged. Basically once you are finished with the [criminal justice] system, like once you are on your release date they can't help you and *that is why I kept going back so many times because I had nowhere to go.*

Meaningful and Sustainable Employment

Criminalized women are among the most disadvantaged in terms of marketable job skills and levels of education. It is women's position within the capitalist patriarchal structure, rather than the inadequacy of women as individuals, that accounts for their poverty and unemployment. As we know, joblessness is a key correlate of crime (DeKeseredy et al., 2003). However, even people with full-time jobs who work for the minimum wage are paid to be poor. A recent series of radio programs profiling the economic realities of minimum wage workers in Canada emphasized some well-known trends, including the gender wage gap; the correlation between education and earnings; the concentration of women in low-paid, part-time employment; and the impossibility of surviving in any Canadian urban centre on minimum wage earnings (Canadian Broadcasting Corporation [CBC] 2004).

In Canada in 2001, more than half of the working poor (some 900,000 individuals) who remained trapped in low-paid work were older women and/or women who had only high school education or less. These women are more likely to be working part-time for small, non-unionized organizations. Furthermore, although the gender gap for income has been narrowing for the past twenty years or so, a woman was still earning 64 cents for every dollar a man was making. Women today account for almost two-thirds of Canada's minimum-wage workers. In 2003, one in twenty-five Canadian employees worked at or below the minimum wage set by their respective provinces. Four out of ten of these minimum-wage workers did not have a high school diploma – pointing to a direct correlation between education and income. Furthermore, one of the hurdles that the working poor in Canada face is the so-called casualization of the work place, a term used to describe the move towards part-time and temporary employment; women consistently occupy positions in the casual labour force which lack benefits such as sick leave, holidays, and medical coverage (CBC 2004).

For single mothers, access to even a poverty-level minimum-wage jobs has been blocked by the absence of a national daycare program. Daycare costs have increased dramatically in Canada over the past ten years. The working poor are 'nickel and dimed' (Ehrenreich 2001) into extreme poverty and substandard living conditions, and then they are made to feel, according to neoliberal ideologies, that 'being poor is a crime in and of itself' (Gilliom 2001: 44).

As Eaton (1993: 71) has pointed out in her study of women after prison, men's and women's jobs are segregated both horizontally (into different occupations) and vertically (with women occupying subordinate positions within the same occupation). Women's paid employment tends to be clustered around low-paying service work. In my study, gender-based job segregation is evident in the context of government-sponsored parole release job programs. Sarah talked about an extension of this gendered division of labour at the local level:

Like they had that place out there in Bull Arm, and in each division they had so many places reserved for men on parole for work. Now they were out there making a killing. They were good-paying jobs. Now what's here for women to go at? Nothing. The government should fund something for women when they come out [of prison] if they want to go back to school and they get paid while they are going to school. And I mean good pay. Bring them above the poverty line. But there is nothing here for women when you got a police record. Like if women came out and had a chance to go to Bull Arm to work and someone to help with their kids, they would make money, enough to keep them going. They would be able to pay their rent, buy their groceries.

Charmaine commented on gender role stereotypes that presume a male wage-earner:

[There need to be] some kind of work programs for women. Somebody should be able to have something to put women into some kind of job program or something. I know if I had been working I would have never been in prison. Definitely not. They have them for men but not a damn thing for women. They thinks that men are the main breadwinners.

No doubt, the possession of a criminal record further narrows a woman's chances of securing employment. Corrina remarked on her experience interviewing for a minimum-wage job:

A criminal record makes it hard to get a job. I got interviewed for a job down at the mall before Christmas last year. I never even heard back. Not so much as a 'No, we have everyone hired.' I just stood out different from the rest of the girls. It was a group interview. I stood out more than anyone else there. I was more nervous.

Charmaine commented on the necessity of employment not only as an economic end but for psychological well-being: 'What would keep me out would be work. It's a big thing. Everybody needs work. People with criminal records, they can't get jobs. If [only] there was some kind of job program for people coming out of prison. Idle hands only gets you in trouble.' Jennifer described the quandary that she faced when searching for employment and the decision whether to disclose her criminal record: 'You try to get a job and first thing they ask is if you have a record. I was going around for about a week trying to get my cheques changed, and I couldn't get it changed because I didn't have a picture ID ... I had to show them my parole card!' Unable to secure employment, Sarah talked about alternative measures for making ends meet on the inadequate social assistance rates. In face of the enduring reality of poverty, options are severely limited:

I live on my own. I got to take in two girls to help me pay the rent so I can go out and buy groceries and a new pair of jeans, sneakers, gym clothes, or a new winter coat for them [children]. It's not really expensive but something they would like. A single woman would never make it in an apartment [on her own]. You need help. If you can't get help, and if you get someone to come and stay with you like a boyfriend or something to help you out then they cut your cheque off because he's got money. That's not fair. This is you. You are not married to this man. He is not obligated to give you anything.

Olivia highlighted her lack of marketable skills, given that the majority of her life has been consumed with the unpaid and undervalued labour of child care:

If I could work instead of going back home and sitting on my ass all day. But I mean even if there were jobs out there, how many people in the name of God are going to take somebody who got no experience of work? That's all I knows is looking after babies and looking after homes, right?

The well-documented lack of gender-based supports for women in prison is replicated on the outside. Because of the·lack of gender-specific programming, women are often mandated to attend counselling programs that are centred on the needs of male offenders. Rebecca, who has been convicted of property offences, has attended anger management sessions each and every time she has returned to the outside. She observed the futility of such programs in addressing her criminality: 'I don't want to keep doing the same garbage I've been doing. I am wasting my time and their time by going to a program that I've already done ten times. It done nothing for me.' Valerie remarked on the lack of women-only programming on the outside and her forced attendance at group counselling sessions on sexual abuse – which clearly target male sex offenders and not their victims:

They [Transition House] take women coming out of prisons. And they take sex offenders and everything for God's sake. Why should I give credit to them for helping me when they didn't? And since I am doing well they all look at you different, and I ain't paranoid either. When you're well you see things that others who are medicated or half out of it don't see. And all their groups are addictions and abuse and that's it. There's nothing like journalling, which helped me a lot. I had to do that myself.

Yvonne also criticized programs that include both sex offenders and victims and the level of anxiety that she experienced in this mixed group:

They have a lot of women coming there with abuse issues. I found it very difficult when I first went there [mandatory counselling group], and you are in a group and you have sex offenders sitting across from you, and you had to try and talk about abuse. I met one guy up there who was a sex offender and staff told him to lie. They just wanted to get the contracts for both groups. So what are they running? Do they take sex offenders or don't they?

The availability of culturally specific programming for criminalized women is non-existent. Nicole described the only Native-run program in St John's and the experience she had there:

> I went up there [to the Native Friendship Centre] for two minutes. They were okay when they were on Casey Street. The doors were unlocked and you could go and have a smoke and a coffee. But once they got a new place on Waterford Bridge Road, their staff are behind closed doors and they have the glass in the window. It don't seem like no friendship centre. I dropped up and dropped back out again. It seems worse than prison in there. It is supposed to be a friendship centre. It is not supposed to be run like a frigging prison.

Victoria summed up the current fiscal situation and the off-loading of state-run programming onto local agencies that lack the human and fiscal resources to effectively deal with the individual populations that they are mandated to serve:

> There's not enough services out there. Emmanuel House is swamped. They cannot take everyone at one time. People on wait lists. There's not enough things for people. And inside there is nothing. It's ridiculous. If they want to save money from people doing crime put something in place to help people. I guess they have got to keep their jobs, too. Staff and jobs and buildings.

Rachael is a young single mother. She commented on one particular program, which is geared towards the educational and financial needs of single parents, that she independently sought out at the expiration of her parole:

> If they had more programs, like SPAN [Single Parents Association of Newfoundland]. At least you are doing something productive that makes you feel good about yourself. Like I know myself once I start paying bills, like when I paid my phone bill like that was the best feeling I ever had, compared to having him [her son]. It makes me feel like I am doing something in society. I am not depending on other people to get what I need. I am doing it on my own even though the money is coming from them [SPAN]. Now that I am getting a bit of money from them [SPAN], going to classes, and I got a babysitter, there is a possibility [of staying out]. It just makes me feel good.

Yvonne pointed out the lack of trained professionals and gender-appropriate spaces on the outside to effectively deal with the myriad issues facing women:

> I really feel that women should have their own place [apart from men]. It's a separate issue. You could relapse for sure in a place with sex offenders. I think men got more facilities anyways. They've got a couple of places already. What's a woman got to come out to? Nothing. You also need counsellors who understand. Not just professionals. A degree is no good without [lived experience]. A degree is only a piece of paper. You need to understand to be able to help them, to walk in their shoes. Some of them haven't got a clue where I am coming from. I don't want to talk to someone like that. It is very frustrating.

Local supports to address the systemic issues facing criminalized women are notably absent. Rebecca has found that programming in and of itself is futile when women are continually faced with issues of cyclical poverty and abuse: 'There is nothing here for women where you have a group on how to stay out. How to live outside. No education groups here at all. You are just being stuck. You are not allowed to go to school. There is not a program here in Newfoundland for shoplifting. Not one.'

Another disturbing trend that was identified by the women in my study is the situation whereby parole releases are denied solely on the basis of the lack of supports available to women on the outside. Kathleen said:

> Out here [in the community] there is nothing. When I had my parole hearing, my parole officer never even recommended me for release because there is nothing out here for women.

Police Surveillance

One major area of concern raised throughout the interviews is police intrusion and surveillance of women post-prison. Often the police are the first agents of the state to impose formal social control. In 2000, two local men (Norman Reid and Darryl Power) with diagnosed mental illnesses were shot and killed within a period of fifty-one days by police officers in Newfoundland. An inquiry later concluded that these so-called incidents were the result of the 'health, social and justice services in this province [which] failed Norman Reid and Darryl Power.' (Luther Inquiry 2003). The report noted that provincial mental health legislation had not been updated since its inception in 1971, thereby making it the oldest Mental Health Act in the country. The inquiry was headed by Judge Luther. Among his key recommendations were the following: establishment of a Mental Health Division of the Provincial Court; a comprehensive new provincial Mental Health Act; stringent criteria for certification to a psychiatric institution; provisions for a community treatment order and conditional leave with appropriate safeguards; additional funding for Health Boards to provide assertive case management of individuals with mental illnesses; establishment of mobile health units to respond to mentally ill persons in crisis; core funding to the local chapter of the Canadian Mental Health Association; and a comprehensive strategy to rid society of the stigma attached to mental illness.

The Luther Inquiry raised a number of key concerns surrounding police involvement in monitoring the whereabouts of prisoners upon release, especially those with mental health diagnoses. Not surprisingly, former prisoners' efforts to stay out of trouble are often inhibited by the constant scrutiny of the police. Sarah explained:

> The police. They are a big part of it. They don't leave you alone. They see you walking along the street, they stop and say, 'What are you at tonight [Sarah]? Are you under any restrictions?' In front of everybody, you know. 'Are you drinking? Are you under any kind of court orders or anything?'

Jamie related first-hand how police interference continues to control her whereabouts and activities:

> Sure I am telling you, I have come out of the shower to run out and answer the phone, and there would be a paddy wagon that would pull in right there [points to the front window] on the wrong side of the road. And me standing up there with a towel around me. There's two men in a paddy wagon staring at me. They [police] were having meetings at the [town hall] for all the break and entries and stuff in the areas and one man I was renting from told me he heard horror stories and people told him not to associate with me.

Corrina commented on attempting to avert the glare of the police. To say the least, she distrusts the authorities.

> They [the police] put the spotlights on us. They would come down the

road and slow down at our place and all heads are turning and looking. Police will not leave us alone. If you do time and you come out and if there is a similar type of crime [to the ones I committed] they will always go back to that person. Even if it was ten years later. Now they are trying to get this DNA in for people who done high crimes. I don't agree with that. They could turn around and plant a hair sample or anything and there are bad god-damned cops.

Leanne articulated her frustration over rehabilitation efforts inside prison that are then contradicted on the outside by state control agents:

Police don't say you got your time done and that you paid back your debt to society. That's what it's all supposed to be about. What groups you got inside the prison they don't know about. Anger management and people skills and you could be the best kind of a person. They don't know, and they don't want to know. They just treat you the same way they did when they picked you up for doing whatever you done. And that's the way it is.

Maggie told of the persistent reminders of being an 'ex-con' when it comes to dealing with the police: 'A few weeks ago I had someone break into my house and I called the police. They didn't even come by. They said they searched the area and that was it. They didn't even come by to take a statement.' Ironically, Emily recounted how police relations have recently changed for her now that she is 'on the other side of the law':

I couldn't pull the car out of the driveway without them [police] pulling me over. At one point one night I had been out with a friend of mine at two or three o'clock in the morning and they had me hauled in. There was a time when I laid a complaint against an officer and generally if you lay a complaint against one of them they are all over you. I can get along with them now because I am in this position [of responsibility]. Sometimes I think it is hilarious. The same cops who were trying to arrest me are trying to work with us [laughs]. It's nice to know that when they come here they won't be drawing guns.

Police scrutiny and interrogation extends beyond the women themselves to their families. In Sarah's case, her teenage children are targeted by the police based on her past criminal history, thereby perpetuating the cycle of police interventions:

I was sentenced to the armed robbery – two and a half years. Then there was an armed robbery [later] in this area and so they [police] come in and busted my door in the morning and I am there and the youngsters are there. The door falls in and knocks my youngster over a flight of stairs and my son is up against the wall trying to catch his breath. I said, 'Get away, leave me alone. That is my child. There is something wrong with him. He does not know you. He needs his mother. Leave me alone.'

Attempts to 'go straight' are often truncated by the police and private security who keep a watchful eye on many of the women who have reported histories of theft: 'When I go to the mall all the floorwalkers knows me and I gets followed around everywhere I goes. When I go down on George Street all the police officers knows me even though I don't remember them. I got more of a chance of getting caught or arrested.'

For many women who have a psychiatric illness, their first encounters in a crisis on the outside are with the police. Therefore, the police play a significant role in determining whether a woman is taken to a psychiatric hospital or back into custody. Jennifer described a recent experience:

Like when the cops came here the other night, and the [respite] worker wanted me to go the hospital. I wasn't after sleeping for four days, and I was really agitated, and I didn't want to go to the hospital because I was afraid they would say, 'Oh, look who is back.' Apparently, they came into the hospital to visit me, my workers, the same ones that called the police. When they first arrived here the first thing they said to me is, 'Get your boots on. We are going to the lock-up.' I said, 'Why are we going to the lock-up? I know I have to go and see someone but why do I have to go to the lock-up?'

The labelling process invoked by the criminal justice system complicates an ongoing reintegrative struggle for many women. Sarah talked about the carryover effects of a criminal label on the outside:

If you went to court on a shoplifting charge with me for the same thing you would get probably probation and a fine and you are gone home. I would get time and I would not get bail. Because of my name. Because of my name [my kid] is up in Whitbourne now and he is not able to get bail now, because of me.

Renegotiating Interpersonal Relationships

Interpersonal relationships play a major role in women's lives after they are released from prison (Eaton 1993; O'Brien 2001). Primary relationships discussed here include those with immediate biological family members, intimate partners, and professional staff.

Familial Relations

Very few women in my sample have supportive family networks. This can be traced back to a number of sources already discussed, including histories of physical and sexual abuse by family members, dissolution of kinship relations upon entering foster care arrangements, and the breakdown and disassociation of family relations experienced upon entering prison and other institutions. For the small number of women who had strong and supportive family networks, this proved to be an invaluable source of support at all stages of their criminalization, especially when it came to 'making it' on the outside. Sarah is a young single mother, and she recognizes family support as being vitally important in her life:

> Oh my God. I don't know how I would get through it without my own family. They should have a program for women in prison who have no family where you can adopt their child just by sending them so much money a month. Adopt them, do crafts, spend time with them. Everyone needs to have someone to care for them.

Jessica also spoke about the importance of family supports throughout her life:

> I would never have been able to do it without my family. I mean I had excellent, excellent, excellent family support all the way through. I had two children before I was twenty years old. I mean, you know, I had a lot of help through the years. I was very fortunate. Many times if I wanted to just leave and go away for the weekend, I could go. I didn't have to worry about having to find a babysitter. I didn't even have to make arrangements. If I wanted to go, I just went. And that was my escape too. I was lucky for that, you know. I find some people get stressed out with youngsters. They can't go. They can't do anything. I was lucky enough that I could.

Valerie, too, recognized the invaluable support that she received from her foster family once she 'went straight':

> I just started to get my family back when I changed my life. My adopted mom is back in my life. I got my sister who came to visit me two years ago. I got my son. My foster parents have been in my life. They have been there since I was seventeen. They found it hard when I changed my life. They didn't want nothing to do with me. They found it very difficult because I wasn't there. They were always there when I was in a crisis, like if I needed money they had money for me.

Positive familial relationships are a major factor that differentiated the women who 'made it' on the outside from those who continue to cycle back and forth into prison or other institutions. Conversely, for those women for whom institutionalization has played a long-standing and prevalent role in their lives, the absence of positive family supports and role modelling is often a reality. Corrina talked about her long-standing troubled relationship with her mother:

> It wasn't good [relations with her mother], and it's still not. Sometimes I gets angry. Sometimes I won't answer the phone [when Mom calls]. It's like I haven't got the head space to be sitting down and talking to this woman without getting angry, and I don't want to be getting angry at her either. There was never an 'I love you' or anything like that. I am thirty-three years old now. I don't need it now. I could care less.

Jennifer completely lost contact with her family of origin upon entering a psychiatric institution at the age of fourteen:

> My family turned on me for a lot of years. Matter of fact, I didn't even know my mother was dying. They couldn't locate me. They didn't know where I was living or nothing. It was fluke that one of the nurses working in at the hospital that was working in on my unit that week, and she and I were talking, and when she went home she heard they were looking for me. By the time I got home my mother was already dead.

Yvonne described the initial contact with her mother upon her release from prison:

> I got on the bus on July 13th to come home, got stranded in Halifax, ran

out of money there. I stayed at a shelter in Halifax. The churches paid my way across on the boat to Port-aux-Basques. I stayed there overnight, and then the Salvation Army paid my way by bus into town. When I got off the bus I never had a cent to get a taxi or nothing. It was pouring rain, and I mean pouring. I got this taxi driver to dispatch the office and call Mom to see if she had enough money for a cab to get over there. She said she didn't have enough money to pay for a cab. Can you imagine that?

Intimate Relationships

Intimate relationships are often a major source of turmoil and abuse in women's lives. Corrina has been out of prison for over a year now. She talked about her current relationship:

I fuck up relationships big time. I am in one again now with a guy I have known for thirteen years. He's at the halfway house. I don't know how that's going to work out. I'm not going to get my heart right gung-ho into it because I have been there and back with him a hundred times before. When I wasn't in jail, he was. It's a big cycle. So we're trying it now and see what happens.

Intimate relationships are often characterized by abuse. Yvonne described her history of relationships with men:

All the relationships I've been in [with men] have been abusive one way or another. Abuse of drugs, abuse of alcohol, abuse of relationships, mental abuse and physical abuse. Money-wise, everything. It's been a big cycle of abuse every which way except for sexual, that's the only one. It's over and over and over again. I guess where I never had a father figure. I never met my father until I was twenty-one. So it was just this thing about needing the male companionship. It was just like I had to have it.

Corrina recounted an experience that she had with her former boy-friend upon entering prison:

I lost everything [when I went to prison]. [A friend] went down and took what she could, like my daughter's bed and stuff. But then the guy I was going out with at the time went down and had a big old party and decided to take my cheque and change it. He was a nice guy, but he was an alco-holic. He drank too, too much – but he was a nice guy other than that. And he changed my cheque and got charged with fraud. He called me a couple of months later. I got his number and used it to run up his phone bill. So when his phone bill was $700 I said, 'Here's a return for the favor.' (Laughs.) So I got my money back one way or another.

Some women, albeit a very few, described supportive intimate relationships as a major source of assistance throughout their prison terms and, consequently, upon their return back home. Victoria told of the support that she receives from her same-sex partner:

The only supports I really have is my partner and my foster parents because [the halfway house] don't give a fuck. They are just as bad as anybody else. When you are doing well you notice things that you wouldn't normally see if you weren't well. When you are medicated you don't see anything. I couldn't even talk right when I got out of prison. My speech was very slurred. They had me blown up on pills. I didn't have clothes. I didn't have food when I first got out. I had no money, and what I did have I spent it on drugs. I would never have done it without her [partner].

Rebecca attributed her sobriety, in large part, to the support of her partner: 'Drugs are not an issue for me anymore. Now, before when I first started I was really nervous and I used to take Valium. I got off of them. I'd say if it wasn't for her [partner's] support, I would probably be back on my pills.' Jennifer acknowledged the emotional support of her partner. She was also aware that this does not go far enough in dealing with the economic realities of poverty that many criminalized women continue to face upon release:

I get support from [my partner] and the kids. But he is getting sick of it. I keeps telling him there is nothing I can do about it. I am not going to sit here and be hungry. No way.

Histories of physical and sexual abuse often leave women struggling to develop trusting and egalitarian relationships with men. Victoria described this ongoing cycle:

Relationships is big thing. You've always got to have something. Being so dysfunctional all your life, and being so screwed up from your background, I guess you always got to have something there even if you are not doing so well. You are always getting involved in something negative.

Which I am doing now because I am in this relationship. It is not good because it could land me right back in jail. I know that. I see that. I do understand it. I am trying to get out of it slowly.

Same-sex relationships are not exempt from the difficulties involved in trying to cope with histories of abuse. Victoria reflected on her current relationship:

All [my relationships have been] negative. Even this one is negative. This is not a healthy relationship. We have been in it a year in February. A very unhappy relationship. We broke up and we're kind of still seeing each other. I don't know. It's not a healthy relationship. I've got to make some decisions. I can't be around this.

For many single mothers, relationships with their former partners are marked by a complete lack of financial and emotional support in caring for their children. Sarah talked about the struggle of trying to make it without any support:

[Former husband] is here in town but he does not take part in the children's lives whatsoever. He has four daughters of his own [and he can't even take care of them]. At Christmas time I used to have to shop for them, and I wouldn't have money enough to get it, but I would make sure they had enough and they had what they wanted [by shoplifting].

Professional Relations

For many women with a long-standing history of institutionalization, primary relationships develop with professional staff, for example, probation and parole officers, psychiatric staff, or counsellors. However, these relationships are not always positive, and they are often characterized by a level of mistrust, in large part because of their transient and situational nature: professional relationships and issues of confidentiality, which are often surrendered in a prison or locally run centre, can make women feel uncomfortable about sharing aspects of their lives in this setting. These relationships often hinge on the duty that professional staff may have to report information that they think indicates a threat – to the women themselves or to others. This is very much the case in an institutional setting, where front-line staff double as 'keepers' and counsellors. Jamie described this complication:

Well it would be all right if they [corrections staff] asked you what was bothering you and try and help you about that, but it seems like they are always asking you how you feel. I don't know. They just don't get to the bottom of the problem. Never did get to the bottom of mine anyways ... And I never did get any help ... [Psychiatrist] comes in here [the prison] but I don't find they help a big lot. I've been seeing a psychiatrist from the time I was seventeen until I was about thirty-two. And I have been in and out of psychiatric wards all that time, and doctors never ever helped me much.

Jennifer had established a close relationship with her parole officer over a number of years. She described how the completion of her parole and therefore this relationship affected her emotionally:

I tell you what else was really funny and helped me complete my parole without even so much as a violation of any kind was my parole officer. Like she would come down, and me and her would go out for a coffee and a drive somewhere. A couple of days before I finished parole and she came down and said, 'Look I am filling up the tank and anywhere you wants to go we are going. Okay?' I said, 'I tell you where I want to go and that's to Ferryland to see my nephew's grave. I have not been there in fifteen years.' And she said, 'Okay.' [Then] she said, 'You know, I have to come down and say good-bye to you.' I felt like I lost my best friend. I really did.

Maggie also described the close relationship that she developed with her former parole officer:

I got out of the parole system three years ago. I really cared about [my parole officer]. I learned how to read and write all over again just for her. I would write her poems. I got into painting and drawing pictures for her. She didn't even appreciate it by writing me back. I can't handle being abandoned. That makes me really hurt. When people go out of my life like that, it really hurts. She had a big impact on my life.

Jennifer noted the significant differences that positive relationships with professional staff can make in a person's life:

There was this one guard in Springhill, and no matter what the other guards said, she always treated me really good. If any clothes came in, she always made sure I had first choice at it. Even the day I was getting released on parole she was the one that brought me to the airport and stayed with me until my flight was ready, and stuff like that. Me and her had a long talk, and she told me if you goes federal any more you knows you are going for a long time. So I think that is one of the things that is probably keeping me straight.

Prolonged dependency on professional staff is a major part of the lives of women who have either been institutionalized or do not have any other supports in terms of family or partnerships. Jennifer explained her fear of losing this support network, built up over a number of years:

> I know that [my home care supports will get reduced], but I also know that it will not be a shock. It will be something that is gradual. You know, eventually I have to get used to being on my own again. One thing I am worried about that could put me back in again is what kind of relationship I am going to have with this new probation officer. Am I going to get along?

Maggie also talked about the need for professional supports on the outside to assist women who have been confined in institutions for most of their lives:

> We need counsellors and people to come in to slowly integrate us into society. When we do learn how to do some of these things again, we need people to show up periodically. You can't just abandon us altogether. Before that person goes away on us, slowly get us used to another person. We just can't be left on our own. Certain people can do it. But people like me, I know cannot make it on our own, by ourselves. I am too institutionalized. For the rest of my life and the rest of my days. If not, people like me will spend the rest of [our lives] in prison.

Olivia expressed her opinion of psychiatric and/or counselling professionals and the artificial and imbalanced environment created between the 'helper' and the 'helped':

> I would love to sit down with a psychiatrist. But what turns me off is you go into this fancy office, here they are wearing this fancy suit, crossing their legs and their shoes so shiny, and here they are with a little marker in their hand scribbling down a few little words, and then, 'I will see you next week.' They thinks they knows what you are going through, but they don't because they have never been through it.

Maggie echoed a concern that was raised by several women about the medication of their problems by psychiatric staff:

> [What I need to stay out], well, for one thing, when I do get out is to find help for one thing. Maybe join ... AA. Go to doctors. The ones who are going to help me. Not the ones who are going to give me a pile of pills, fifteen minutes, mark down a couple of words, and 'We'll see you next week.'

Olivia made the point that male professionals, either in prison or on the outside are incapable of empathizing with her history of sexual and physical abuse, thereby providing little help in dealing with her past abuse and little guarantee that she will not return to prison:

> I can't say I won't be back. I can't say that. I am not going to say I am not going to go out there and hit the bottle, right? But on the other hand, I am going to ask God to keep me strong. I am going to ask the good Lord to keep me strong. I am definitely going to ask the Lord to keep me strong. But I think once I gets out in that place in town [Transition House], once I'm there and they are talking with me. It's like to me, to tell you the truth, if I had a powerful staff person, like a female, I think she would understand me a little bit more. She is more warmer, you know. But with a man, it's like he's there with crossed legs and (laughs) it's like he don't understand right.

Immediate challenges facing women upon their release from prison are undoubtedly important to overcome. However, once these goals have been met, the struggle is by no means over, and obstacles to staying out remain. The next chapter further breaks down the challenges that women face in trying to stay out of prison once these more immediate targets have been met.

7 State and Localized Controls

You are never out of the system once you're in it. You are never ever out of it. I don't care what anyone says. Like I am out of it now but I am still not out of it. I am still doing time [on the outside].

Jennifer

The major finding of this book centres on the layers of social controls that characterize the lives of criminalized women. The more layers of formal state control that a woman has encountered prior to her coming into prison, the less likely she is to break away from the criminal justice system upon release. Furthermore, institutional responses to criminalized women are replicated at the local level, where transcarceral strategies of social control push the so-called clients of the criminal justice system 'from one section of the help-control complex to another' (Lowman, Menzies, and Palys 1987: 9). By managing and supervising criminalized populations on the outside, the penal apparatus expands to include state controls (psychiatry and mental health, welfare, child protection) and local controls (home care, mandatory programming, and residential centres). In the case of local initiatives, the offloading of state responsibilities in the name of economic prudence has meant a scramble by local groups to obtain core government funding to sustain their operations. This means a co-opting of local organizational missions and principles to accommodate state-imposed policies and practices.

Social Control and Transcarceration

The term *social control* has been bandied about in the sociological literature for decades. It sometimes appears as a 'term to cover all social processes to induce conformity' (Cohen 1985: 2). These social processes include education, family relations, and peer-group interactions. Carlen notes that social control is a vacuous term implying anything from conspiracy theories that view every social practice as part of the social control process to a very narrow definition referring only to the state's official mechanisms of controlling crime (2003: 119). In other sociological interpretations, the term is applied to all state-sponsored social policies, including health and welfare, and it is strictly confined to the coercive apparatus of the state. Cohen defines social control as somewhere in between these two poles and more general than the 'formal legal-correctional apparatus for the control of official crime and delinquency.' Social controls are 'those organized responses to crime, delinquency and allied forms of deviant and/or socially problematic behaviour which are actually conceived of as such, whether in the reactive sense (after the putative act has taken place or the actor been identified) or in the proactive sense (to prevent the act). These responses may be sponsored directly by the state or by more autonomous professional agents in, say, social work and psychiatry. Their goals might be as specific as individual punishment and treatment or as diffuse as 'crime prevention, "public safety" and "community mental health" (1985: 3.)'

While I concur with Cohen on the necessity of broadening the purview of social control elements outside the criminological domain, I advocate a more encompassing definition that extends itself beyond the official and formal delivery agents of the state. In particular, a gender-based analysis of social control must be invoked. There is nothing coincidental about the nature and types of social controls that are exerted on girls and women who end up as the targets of formal penal controls brought about by the criminal justice system. It extends far beyond these parameters. Although much of my analysis is premised on Cohen's broader interrogations, gender remains at the forefront of my analysis surrounding women's involvement with formal control agents. A grounding in the work of social control theorists acts as a starting point for my discussions of not only women entangled in the criminal justice system, but also of women 'at risk' of criminalization and of women for whom the criminal justice system represents just one more force along a broader continuum of controls that have pervaded their entire lives.

Drawing on the work of Carlen, an alternative lens for analysing the different types of controls experienced by women is invoked through the term *antisocial control*, which is defined as 'a generic term for a variety of malign institutionalized practices that may either set limits to individual action by favouring one set of citizens at the expense of another so as to subvert equal-opportunities-ideologies in relation to gender, race, and class (or other social groupings), or (in societies without equal-opportunities ideologies) set limits to individual action in ways that are antisocial because they atrophy an individual's social contribution on the grounds of either biological attributes or exploitative social relations' (2003: 119). The major advantage of adopting this antisocial definition of control is that it takes into account the ideological, political, and economic milieu in which control is exerted. In particular, it draws on control agents outside the purview of the criminal justice system when analysing the (anti)social control of women. These sites of control include: (1) the 'antisocial family,' wherein historically, women are expected to subject themselves first and foremost to the family. The powerful ideology that 'good mothers make good families make good societies' and that the family, in turn, 'must forever be at the service of the military, the markets, and the man' extends the discussions of control over women's lives; (2) the 'antisocial state' is interconnected to women's assumed domesticity, wherein defiance of these expected roles subjects women to exclusionary and more formal measures of obedience, and; (3) 'antisocial masculism,' which is achieved by the physical exclusion of women from public spaces, public institutions, and workplaces, managed primarily through law, the economy, and tradition (Carlen 2003: 122–4).

Additionally, a further subjection of women has been achieved through beauty myths and body image norms that target conformity. For women unable or unwilling to cope, there have been the (overprescribed) tranquilizers and the (oversubscribed) mental hospitals. Official regulatory agencies such as the courts and prisons are but the end result of the antisocial targeting of women's conformity that is achieved through various other converging social institutions (Carlen 2003: 125). Keeping these other antisocial control mechanisms in full view, the power of the courts and laws to then criminalize women's so-called disobedience must be placed into this wider context. In adopting an antisocial control framework, however, it is to the grounding of 'traditional' control theories that the deconstruction of reintegration, decarceration, and transcarceration within the criminal justice system takes place.

Central to the analysis of 'community-based reforms,' which have been implemented over the past several decades in both the criminal-justice and mental-health spheres, convincing arguments based on mounting empirical evidence point to net-widening in these systems. Decarceration attempts have failed to bring about their desired goals of closing down institutions and locating 'clients' in their communities: 'Instead of destructuring, however, the original structures have become stronger; far from any decrease, the reach and intensity of state control have been increased; centralization and bureaucracy remain; professions and experts are proliferating dramatically and society is more dependent on them; informalism has not made the legal system less formal or more just; treatment has changed its forms but certainly not died' (Cohen 1985: 37).

Scull has outlined the historical context of the decarceration movement that took place in mental hospitals and prisons during the 1960s and 1970s, noting that decarceration is simply 'shorthand for a state-sponsored policy of closing down asylums, prisons and reformatories. Mad people, criminals, and delinquents are being discharged or refused admission to the dumps in which they have been traditionally housed. Instead they are left at large, to be coped with "in the community"' (1977:1).

There is widespread disagreement among policymakers and the public about what the term *community* actually encompasses and very little empirical support that it is effective in meeting its intended goals of rehabilitation, cost-savings, and increased humanity. In practice, community-based alternatives are ripe with euphemisms, such as 'personal care homes' and 'treatment centres,' which effectively camouflage the reality of people's precarious existence on the outside. Scull maintains that 'decarceration thus forms yet one more burden heaped on the backs of those who are most obviously the victim of our society's inequities. And it places the deviant in those communities least able to care for or cope with them' (1977: 2).

The shift to deinstitutionalize mentally ill patients and prisoners is driven by advanced capitalist market economies seeking to disaggregate social control models that they find far too costly; by the advent of the therapeutic millennium and psychoactive drugs; and an alleged concern with the more humane provision of so-called treatment services on the outside. Decarceration efforts have been a failed attempt to shut down, or even reduce the size and expanse of institutions: 'An apparently radical decarceration strategy ends up only shifting custody from the state to local level and becoming a revenue sharing carve-up between local agencies' (Cohen 1985: 96).

The resistance strategies employed by middle- and upper-class communities to housing the 'mad' and the 'bad' in their neighbourhoods have forced the situating of these makeshift and halfway residences in transient, deleterious, and deteriorated urban locales. Treatment under these conditions of restraint is no more conducive or empowering than that in the rightly criticized confines of the institution. From a purely economic stance, reducing expenditures by means of deinstitutionalization means doing less with less. The treatment services and housing arrangements made available to former psychiatric patients and former prisoners, for example, are heaped onto the private sector, largely free of state regulation and inspection, and are more often than not pressured into conforming to state-based ideologies. This amounts to little more than the 're-packaging of misery' and it is 'scarcely surprising to learn that decarceration in practice has displayed remarkably little resemblance to liberal rhetoric on the subject. Indeed, the primary value of that rhetoric ... seems to have been its usefulness as ideological camouflage, allowing economy to masquerade as benevolence and neglect as tolerance' (Scull 1977: 152).

Cohen makes clear the extent of the co-optation of community by decarceration strategies in stating that 'intervention comes earlier, it sweeps in more deviants, is extended to those not yet formally adjudicated and it becomes more intensive. And all of this takes place in agencies co-opted into the criminal justice system (but less subject to judicial scrutiny), dependent on system personnel for referrals and using more or less traditional treatment methods' (1985: 53). The boundaries between prison and the community are ever increasingly blurred: 'it is by no means easy to know where the prison ends and the community begins or just why any deviant is to be found at any particular point ... [t]he term community treatment has lost all descriptive usefulness except as a code word with connotations of "advanced correctional thinking" and implied value judgements against the "locking up" and isolation of offenders' (ibid.: 58). The community then becomes the site of offloading by the state and the further blurring of the boundary between private and public space. To survive, local organizations must count on state funding to maintain their operations and as a consequence become co-opted by and absorbed into the formal state apparatus. What is clear is 'that a probable outcome of this blurring is ... the creation of a hidden custodial system, under welfare or psychiatric sponsorship, which official delinquency statistics simply ignore. This is the real, awful secret of community control. Not the old closely guarded secrets of the penitentiary (the brutality, the chain gangs, solitary confinement). These things occur in the community – and this is, by any measure, progress. The secret is a much less melodramatic one: that the same old experts have moved office to the community and are doing the same old things they have always done. Once again, we do not know what they are doing, not because they are hidden behind walls but because they are camouflaged as being just ordinary members of the community' (ibid.: 62–75).

Much has been written on the institutionalization and decarceration of mental patients (see, e.g., Goffman 1961; Scull 1977), providing powerful evidence of the stakes of professional interest groups and the growth of whole industries in whose favour it is to keep the numbers high. 'Social control entrepreneurship' (Warren 1981) describes the rationale behind this expansion: 'To keep your job, to justify your existence, to attract grants and subsidies, you must keep on expanding' (Cohen 1985: 167). In commenting on the continuum of controls exhorted over psychiatric patients, Cohen writes: 'The mental-health network contains its own hard-soft bifurcation exactly parallel to that in the criminal justice system. At the core remains the classic asylum, relegated by the ideology of community to a dumping ground for chronic clients and favouring drug and behaviour therapy. In the next circle comes the community mental-health services and clinics, taking in a mixture of the old decarcerated patients and an increasing number of newer cases brought in by the net-widening ideology of preventive psychiatry and community mental health. These patients receive a mixture of drug therapy and traditional but watered down psychodynamic modalities' (ibid.: 153).

Net-widening is at the centre of the social control network and is characterized as an endless tautology of recycling clients back and forth from one so-called help system to another. Once one is entangled in this web of state-sponsored control, it becomes nearly impossible to break free from the host of sponsors who maintain their stakes in keeping the cycle revolving: 'Control leads to more control ... Almost the entire alternatives, diversion and community movements can be seen as loop ... new systems being created to deal with the damage done by the old systems, but then inflicting their own kind of "damage" from which clients have to be further saved, diverted, delabelled or decategorized. Diversion agencies loop clients away from the criminal justice system, then screening procedures have to be developed to loop the "wrong" clients away from the diversion agencies. Theoretically, there is no end to this process' (Cohen 1985: 171–2).

Building upon the tenets of social control theory, transcarceral strategies of social control are characterized by institutional mobility wherein clients of the criminal justice system are pushed from one section of the help-control complex to another (Lowman, Menzies, and Palys 1987: 9). By managing and supervising offenders on the outside, the penal apparatus expands to include welfare, mental health agencies, social services, child protection agencies, educational resources, halfway houses, treatment centres, and so forth: 'Agencies within the criminal justice system might compete over the same potential clientele, or clients might be tracked and retracked between crime, welfare and psychiatric systems ... boundaries between these systems are now less clearly defined and therefore gains and losses are virtually impossible to estimate. The flow occurs in both directions: former offender groups are retracked into welfare or mental health system and previous patients (notably decarcerated mentally ill adults) come into the criminal justice system' (Cohen 1985: 54–5). A transcarceral model of social control builds upon much of the earlier analyses of control theories, but advances the arguments even further. An interpretative framework for transcarceration encompasses 'a peno-juridicial, mental health, welfare and tutelage complex in which power structures can be examined only by appreciating cross-institutional arrangements and dynamics. Thus, "privatization," "decontrol," "deinstitutionalization," "decentralization" and so on, have consequences for security, courts, corrections, probation, parole, welfare and mental health ... For control agents, this means that "control" will essentially have no locus and the control mandate will increasingly entail the "fitting together" of subsystems rather than the consolidation of one agency in isolation from its alternatives' (Lowman, Menzies, and Palys 1987: 9).

Focusing on the manifestations of social control on women, Davis and Faith proceeded from an inherent assumption that mechanisms and rationales of control are gendered and that 'sexist traditions and ideologies are rampant in both the formal and informal spheres of control.' The involvement of the state in controlling the lives of women permeates beyond the institution. Women continue to be penalized for violating traditional sex roles (antisocial control) and for defying the maintenance of social order. Patriarchal relations, which serve as a basis for defining women as 'deviant' in sexually demeaning and dependent ways, include pornography, rape, the sexualization of women's crimes, and prostitution (Davis and Faith 1987: 186). Neoconservative political agendas exert increasingly punitive and institutionalized controls over women for behaviours that counter the gender roles demanded of women and their opposition to these demands: 'When this labelling occurs it neutralizes and obfuscates a political phenomenon by defining it as deviant. To institutionalize opposition in the name of health, welfare, treatment, penalty and public safety is to attempt to silence that opposition' (ibid.: 187). Moreover, certain groups of women are more vulnerable to instutionalized controls than are other women (and men): 'Disobedient or runaway adolescent females, those who are sexually active or pregnant, in violation of husband's or father's wishes, and the "unfit" mother are far more likely to be candidates for intervention than disobedient, runaway, sexually promiscuous, or domestically-abusive males' (ibid.: 172–3). One major arena of intervention into women's lives is through psychiatry and mental health. It is to a discussion of formally sanctioned state agents of control that I now turn.

State Agents of Control

Almost two-thirds of the women in my study who have been 'successful' in avoiding a return to custody within a two-year period are now as tightly entrenched in outside psychiatric and mental health agencies as they were during their stays in prison. They have stayed out of prison, but they are now either resident in a psychiatric hospital or receiving full-time 'respite care' in their homes. Jennifer described what her life has been like since coming out of prison more than three years ago:

> There is nothing I haven't done. I have caught fire to myself. I have jumped off the bridge. I have jumped into St John's Harbour. Ran in front of cars. Basically it comes back to them saying she is looking for attention. So, I might have been able to stay out [of prison] this past couple of years or more, but it hasn't been easy. One day she [the home care worker] came into the house when I was after swallowing down about twenty to thirty bottles of pills. She said to me, 'I am going to have to call the police.' I hauled out the knife and said, 'It is too late to call the police.' She grabbed the knife and cut her finger. And I told her to get out. She went and called the police. They came and charged me with assault causing bodily harm. So, I had a choice. I plead guilty so they put me in at the Waterford Justice Unit. When I got out I told them I didn't want any more home-care workers. And so they weren't happy with me being there by myself, so they put me back into the Waterford, and that's where I was until now.

Yvonne recounted her cycle of psychiatric admissions and the reality that it is through her encounters with the criminal justice system that she has accessed the psychiatric interventions that she needed upon release:

I have over 100 admissions there [Waterford Hospital]. It's hard to break out of that cycle too. That's what happened to me. The mental health system refused me but the prison system couldn't refuse me. That's a fact. It's hard to get some help. I got more help in the prison system than I got in there [Waterford]. I only got abused in there. I never got any help from the Waterford. I got slapped to death and drugged to death and abused. You name it. I have been abused everywhere. They went together anyway, the justice system and the Waterford. That's still to this day.

Maggie talked of the desperation that she feels on the outside and her reliance on mental health agents since coming out of prison:

The Crisis Centre wouldn't talk to me. I was feeling like I didn't belong in the house. I didn't belong at the Waterford. People are telling me death is not the answer and prison is not the answer. I didn't know what the answer was, and I didn't really want to die, so I thought taking the pills would just put me brain dead with just lying in the bed and people seeing my face. Maybe being there in the bed being hooked up to all these fucking wires would make them happy. I still don't feel any happier than I did before prison ... [I feel happy] when people are around. I do feel pretty good after certain people are around. Like the worker who was here today. She pissed me off because she wouldn't loan me money for smokes because she knew you were coming and I was getting paid. I told her I didn't want to take any money from you. I was just delighted that you were coming.

Rebecca spoke of the continuum of mental health that is all too familiar to many criminalized women:

It's much more than the criminal justice system. It's the mental health system. It's social services. It's every other system that plays into it. They got sick of them at the Waterford and shoved them out. They didn't want to deal with them anymore. Those are people who can't cope, and they keep throwing them in jail.

Locking women up under the Mental Health Act is often the first course of action taken by the police in responding to a woman in crisis. Jennifer recalled her most recent experience in this regard:

A few weeks back I went to the hospital to talk to a doctor because I was not feeling well, and I was refused to be seen. And because I was refused to be seen the police came and took me to the lock-up, and I was down there for sixteen hours on a mattress, and that same night I was refused treatment another person was also refused treatment and went over and jumped off the bridge by the Waterford. He's still in critical condition in hospital. The reason the nurse gave me that night on call at the Waterford was that the doctor who was on didn't know me plus they had no beds. She didn't see the purpose of me being seen by a doctor who didn't know me. Then I was taken to St Clare's, and the doctor there would not even come in and see me. So that was when the police came and told me they had no other choice to take me to the lock-up.

Jennifer, having been detained at the lock-up under the Mental Health Act described her resistance to hospitalization:

The police weren't comfortable in me coming back home [from the lock-up] even though I had a worker here with me. The next day a psychiatrist came into the lock-up and told me he was the head of all the hospitals here in the city, and he told me I was going to Waterford. I told him I didn't want to go and he told me I had no choice. He was signing the papers saying I had to go. I said, 'They have no beds.' and he said to me, 'When I want a bed I get a bed.' So 3 o'clock that next afternoon I was admitted to the Waterford.

Jennifer connected the psychiatry-prison continuum that has pervaded her life and that is ongoing even though she has not been to prison in more than three years:

You are never out of the system once you're in it. You are never ever out of it, I don't care what anyone says. Like I am out of it now but I am still not out of it. I am still doing time [on the outside]. Like when I left Springhill no one even gave me the benefit of the doubt that I was going to stay out. And they figured I would be in a breach of parole at any time. I guess I fooled them (laughs). It was no confidence. None at all. I considered it they were there for the cheque and that was it. So, you know, I think if people really took a look at the criminal justice system in Canada they would be shocked. I was in Springhill a year when I caught fire to myself. And then I was transferred to Saskatchewan psychiatric unit.

Despite the fact that Yvonne has been out of prison for two years she is quick to realize that her psychiatric illness can draw her back into the system at any time:

> Like, either way I am getting hauled back in [the system]. It's either the prison or the hospital. I didn't think that was still an issue except for the other night when they came here and they said we are taking you to the lock-up. I did also find out something. It doesn't matter if you are on probation or whatever, they can take you to the lock-up if they think you are trying to hurt yourself or something like that. They are not going to charge you, just hold you. They can only hold you until you are seen by a doctor, and then once you are seen they got no other choice but to either take you to a hospital or release you.

The penal industrial complex is by no means lost on these women who recognize the business of corrections and psychiatry on the outside. Valerie talked about the exploitation of women's labour by some local penal agencies:

> They are not even qualified counsellors. A lot of them up there got Grade 12, and they're doing counselling on abuse! Some of them have a few criminology courses. They've got this thing with $62.50. You've got to work. You've got to get twenty-four hours every two weeks. What's that? About $2.00 an hour? I did catering for them. Here I found out they were paying the staff out of it. We did catering jobs for Mental Health and Justice, and here they were paying staff out of the money that I was earning! And they had this other thing where you stuff envelopes for $5 an hour, but where I was on this twenty-four hour thing they had me doing it and working for half that wage. They get a lump sum payment from the Cancer Society and pocketing that money and just giving the workers the $62.50. Where is all the money going from what we make from catering?

The continuum of dependency on prescription medications is enabled by agents of the criminal justice system who force mandatory drug compliance on women especially those with mental health diagnoses. As Valerie described, monitoring of her intake of drugs prescribed for a diagnosis of bipolar disorder is a condition of her probation. It was only after she had satisfied the terms of her probation order that she managed to renegotiate her own mental health needs according to what she deemed appropriate:

> I had to take my medication. That was a part of my probation. I wasn't

allowed to do drugs, but I was allowed to drink. That makes sense [laughs]. I had to see a probation officer and [Transition] House was involved. I had respite workers, which I didn't want, but I had to have them. They were like pill-pushers ... [W]hen I got off probation I threw my pills in the toilet. I told my probation officer that I was doing that. I had to take my pills or they would have put me back in prison. Part of the conditions.

Supports for women upon their immediate release from prison and while still under the control of probation or parole agencies, in terms of reporting and regular home visits, are diminished as they near the end of their sentences. Maggie regarded this as problematic:

Well first [when I got out of prison], all kinds of counseling. But now I feel like everyone is after abandoning me. I have a lot of physical problems right now. I am worried about not knowing if people are going to be there if I have to get surgery. Right now I am worried because I am that big now that when I go to the washroom I can't even wipe myself, I am that fucking big. I get into the bathtub and I get stuck. I can't even wash myself down below. I can only wash up here. I can't wash my own back. I can barely wash my own head. It makes me depressed. So I run to the institution. The Waterford. Then they make me angry and upset. If they went to grab me and put me in TQ [Therapeutic Quiet], I am liable to hurt someone. I don't want to. I have no plan to hurt nobody. But the next thing you know I am behind bars again. I am not planning to hurt anyone. Honest to God. I love to see people helping. But it's like an adrenaline, it rushes to the head like an empty feeling. A fuzzy feeling in my head. It rushes to my head, and they don't understand that. It's something in my head like a rush goes to my body. It's like my head is working twenty-eight hours out of twenty-four hours. Spinning.

Maggie further elaborated on her recurrent admissions to the psychiatric hospital despite being out of prison for three years:

Frankly what I think [for women in prison] it's a lack of understanding of mental illness. In the past three months I have been in there [Waterford Hospital] nineteen times. And in the past three weeks I have been in there six times. I got out of there yesterday. After OD'ing and they sends me home with more prescription pills! Here, have some more pills!! Do us a favour (and kill yourself). In Newfoundland, you will find that women were institutionalized at a young age at the Waterford. At the Janeway [Children's Hospital]. Doctors overloaded them with medication. Misdiagnosing. Misunderstanding. Not interacting with Child Welfare to take children out of the home at an earlier age when they were being abused. Teachers getting away with covering things up for families.

Jennifer spoke to her ongoing reliance on prescription drugs to medicate the pain of past abuses, which, as she pointed out quite succinctly, do not cease upon the expiration of one's conditional sentence:

Believe it or not for twenty-five or twenty-six years [slashing] was a way, too, of not hurting someone else. It was to hurt myself first. Sad part about this is that for almost a year I didn't know what it was like not to hurt myself and that was the longest time I ever went. All of a sudden last week things just got too much and the first thing I wanted to do was hurt myself. I didn't want to die or anything, I just wanted to feel pain ... There was a lot of things going through my head. I kicked my workers out because I just wanted to be by myself. That was the first night I had spent in the apartment by myself.

Leanne developed an addiction to prescription medications while in prison and now must continue taking her medication to avoid breaching the conditions of her release and being sent back to prison. Having said that, she also recognizes that this is only one piece of the puzzle, with poverty being the main contributor to her past crimes:

[The biggest challenge for me staying out is that] I have to stay on the medication I am on. I have to not drink and not do drugs. Stay away from certain people and make them changes in my life. I'm twenty-five now and this has been the longest time I have been off the drugs. But in terms of shoplifting I think, I know I am going to have to do that again to survive.

A model called 'assertive case management' has been adopted by some local organizations in dealing with criminalized women who have psychiatric labels (Seymour and Greene 2000). This model provides 'intensive supervision to those severely and persistently mentally ill persons whose needs are not met through regular case management' (Luther 2003: 165). Jennifer explained the piloting of this new approach:

I don't know if you know this but I am one of the first ones in Newfoundland that they tried this with [the assertive case management model]. I don't consider myself a criminal half the time. I consider myself sick, and I am being treated like a criminal. But you don't know where to turn. Like my worker couldn't understand the other night why the police came and took me to the hospital. Why would you be glad the police came and got you? Because I knew I was not being violent and I didn't want to hurt them, and I knew I would get there safely and stuff like that. So I mean that was a big thing. That's why I knew then that I wasn't going back. I could have got in that car that night and kicked up a big stink and hit one of those cops. I wouldn't be going to the Waterford. I would be going to the Waterford Justice Unit and then brought to jail. That's the other thing.

Many criminalized women are single mothers, and they are routinely subject to the gaze and intervention of child protection agencies. For some women, child protection is already a well-established layer of social control in their lives prior to their incarceration. For others, their maternal fitness becomes the subject of ongoing intrusion and surveillance after their release. During their period of incarceration, some women have their children placed in temporary foster care arrangements, and mother-child reconciliation becomes the subject of constant monitoring by the state following their release. Not surprisingly, relationships between women and child protection officials are marked by high levels of suspicion and distrust. Olivia, for example, recounted a breach of confidentiality by child protection agents that was used against her at her sentencing:

When I was trying to get my second child back, what they done this time is they went to the Waterford and took out my files. The doctor took out my files without my permission and used that in court. I don't think there was any need of that. I didn't think they was allowed to do that.

Since returning home, Olivia has been subjected to ongoing intrusions by child protection services:

When I had my home and my child that was really a good time. But after one day all that was taken away. They say I was unfit, but they were the ones who drove me there. I mean I used to wash out the clothes twice a day. You could be able to eat off that floor ... Social Services would get calls to come in, and I was getting pissed off. And I had the house spotless. Spotless. And the next thing you know a knock comes on the door. Lord

God. A knock comes on the door and that was Social Services. There was two of them there, and they had a police officer, and they were after getting more calls again. 'What now?' I said. 'Well, we got calls saying your child is sore and you got a hole in the mattress and a bucket beneath the bed.' And I said, 'Lord God.' I got fed up with it and I said, 'Come on in.' By the time the week finished they had the house wrecked. I grabbed the sheets and throwed them on the floor, got the mattress and tore it off. I said, 'look. Do you see a bucket there?' They said no. I took them into the front room. I took off the chesterfield cushions. I said, 'look do you see any buckets there?' Oh, my God, I tell you. It's wicked.

After much ongoing intervention by child protection services throughout her life, Nicole, a middle-aged woman returning to the outside after a three-year federal sentence, placed her children for adoption:

I had my children with me up until 1996, and then I put them up for adoption because I thought that was no life for them. They were in foster care and all that. I thought it was bad enough for the little children to live there and I wanted to give them a chance so I put them up for adoption. At first it was hard, yes. They were in foster care for eight months before they got adopted.

Rachael had her daughter removed from her custody, and she connected this loss to her subsequent criminality:

She [her daughter] is in Child Youth and Family Services. She got apprehended once I got sentenced to two years; she was taken away. She was in temporary wardship with Child Youth at the time, and I went out and they said they were taking her permanently ... of course, I did not agree, and I flipped out and that proved to them again, more or less, that I wasn't capable or wasn't ready to take care of a baby, to be a mother. And of course when they got that order [the apprehension order] that is when I ended up getting in trouble with the law again.

Despite being out of prison for more than two years, upon the birth of her second child Rachael was still subject to routine investigations and home visits by child protection workers:

Child Protection is still involved with me today, of course, because of my past with [my daughter], but they don't have no reason to have any concerns at this point. I have been doing good. I haven't had any trouble with the law. I am basically going to my counselling appointments, and I am showing no signs that I am starting to go back to my old self. Well not to my old self but to them getting in trouble [is my old self]. They don't have no risk concerns at this time.

Mistrust of child protection agents is a common theme among criminalized mothers. Olivia elucidated the basis of this lack of trustworthiness:

Ever since they took those files out and used them against me, I don't feel trustworthy [sic] of them anymore. To take out my files, walk into a court-room, and use it against me and everything. I mean it was strangers in this court. I didn't know nobody. But you know what was strange? I was sitting there in a chair [in the courtroom], and he knew everything about me, but I didn't know nothing about him [refers to the judge]. That was a real blow to me, like when she got up and took out my file and said, '[She] is not capable of looking after her kids because she was sexually assaulted' blah, blah, blah, blah. My God, I said to myself that is supposed to be con-fidential. Maybe things have changed now. That was the [19]70s. I certainly hope they have changed.

Quite similarly to child-protection agents in the nature and extent of their intrusion. welfare officers continue to play an important role in women's lives after their release from prison. Reliance on social assis-tance benefits keeps women entangled in a system of controls wherein regular reporting and check-ups are routine. Jennifer provided one such example of this level of control and intrusion in relation to the monitor-ing of her prescription medications citing the state-endorsed surveil-lance of her drug card as a reason that she is staying out of prison:

One thing that is probably keeping me out is finally, after so many years of going to Social Services and getting a drug card and loading up on pills and overdosing, they [the government] finally realized I am costing them a lot of money. So now my drug card is restrictive, and only my home-care workers can pick up my pills. My pills are locked in a safe, so I cannot even access my pills. So I cannot overdose or anything like that. I guess in a way that is a big benefit.

Monitoring the prescription-medication intake of welfare recipients is a routine occurrence. Additionally, the generation of any income outside the regular welfare payments must be reported to welfare officers. Any change in address or conditions of control by parole services must also be reported to social services. Finally, recipients are subject to unannounced home visits and intrusion by 'welfare cops' employed to detect any fraudulent activities, which include checking up on women to ensure that they are not cohabitating with a male partner. Breach of any one of these stringent regulations could result in criminal charges of welfare fraud and, undoubtedly, this issue is an ongoing source of stress for women.

Local Agents of Control

Community is a term invoked by governments, reformers, feminists, and academics, but seldom do these groups concur on its meaning. Worrall (1997: 3) has argued that 'the term community [h]as become a thoroughly promiscuous word, attaching itself to almost any activity formerly regarded as a responsibility of the state.' The extent to which the so-called community incorporates a number of state agencies (including social services, child protection agencies, the criminal justice system, and mental health agencies) does not necessarily represent a forum for rehabilitation and reintegration. Similarly, the community for women parolees often represents further repression and (in)formal social controls in their lives. Having said that, for women like Yvonne, the level of local supports now in place have come about only as a direct result of her incarceration and entanglement with the criminal justice system:

> The support is out there for me that was never there before. The support is there to help me deal with my anger and issues which was never there before. I had to break the law several times just to get this help. It's pretty bad I had to break the law to be where I am today because of my crimes.

Maggie has been out of prison for more than three years. She talked about the need to differentiate local services for women who have major mental health needs. Because her master status on the outside is that of ex-prisoner, services provisions are based foremost on this label:

> The government should have a place funded for people like me who have a mental illness. They should have people hired for people in the prison system with a mental history. People who have difficulties with the law.

Just regular correctional people don't understand. They need someone hired who understands. I am stable now. I am just after getting out of hospital, and I am on new medication now. Medication helps me stay out of prison is number one. But what if I forget my medication? What if people stop coming around? What if I lose my apartment from getting in with the wrong crowd because I can't say no? What if I start hallucinating, and the new doctors don't believe me? What if I am not representing myself appropriately or inappropriately and they don't know what to believe? They don't know if it is the manipulative side of me coming out or the sick side of me coming out? Sometimes I am manipulative. Sometimes I am telling the truth and sometimes I am not. What do they do if they don't know what to believe? These days I know I am being the most truthful person of my life, and they still don't believe me. What do I have to do? Shed my blood for the system? People like me, all they want to do is lock them up and throw the key away, when initially it is cheaper to hire someone to put in my home than keep them on the street and spending millions upon millions in the prison system and locking them up behind bars.

Jennifer was diagnosed with a major psychiatric illness while in the prison system. She talked about the suspicion that she encounters from the medical profession and her subsequent failure to secure the services of a general practitioner:

One of the biggest problems is that I have been here over two months and they still can't find me a family doctor because as soon as they contact the doctor the first thing they ask them is do I have a psychiatrist? And they said yes and then they say oh she is probably only looking for some narcotics. So I seen my psychiatrist yesterday and the first thing he asked is if I had a family doctor yet and I said no. And he was questioning me and I told him why and he said he would write a letter to verify. I have diabetes so I do have to be monitored by a GP.

For many women like Jennifer, issues of trust and confidentiality are major barriers to seeking counselling and local supports:

One thing about me is that I was being hurt so much. I didn't trust. The trust was gone. Even though people were offering me these opportunities, I was more or less afraid to let it happen. And I got to tell you that I have had my ups and downs even since I have been out. Like I don't think, I am on probation now, and I don't think I will go back to prison because like I have gained so much now that I just don't feel like I need the surroundings now and I did before. It was like a safety place. Right?

Jennifer also noted a sad irony inherent in the end of involvement with the criminal justice system. That is the removal of major support networks that come about as a result of institutionalization:

That's one of the disadvantages of not being in the [criminal justice system] because when I was at Carew Lodge I had family doctors, psychiatrists. [Elizabeth Fry Society staff] was always flying down to see me. Counsellors galore and everything like that. The minute you are finished with the [criminal justice] system, it all goes away.

For many women, particularly those falling into the assertive case management model, life is characterized by the presence of so-called home-support workers' to assist them in their daily rounds. Maggie talked about this trajectory and the dependencies it has created for her:

I won't even go outside now. They [respite workers] expect me to bathe every day. Wash my clothes every day. Clean my house every day. How do they expect me to do that with four fucking [respite] hours? There is no fucking way. I need more hours. More than likely I am going to end up 102B. That's my parole number.

The high turnover in respite staff and the imbalanced professional relationship that exists between worker and client pose a number of problems related to trust and relationship-building. Maggie explained her situation in this regard:

I had [respite care] all along, but it was consistent. Now it's not as consistent anymore. They are hiring new workers. All new faces. Workers are cancelling out at the last minute. They are lying to me. They are deceiving me. When I told the boss a couple of months back that there was a worker talking about me and stealing from me and another client, they didn't believe me but they believed the other client. They say, 'Oh [Maggie] is upset today so we will give her a pack of cigarettes to shut her up.' But I don't want material things. I want someone to sit down and talk to me. Material things mean nothing.

Jennifer provided an example of the rationale for her recent increase in 'support staff': 'The most hours I have ever had in home care is four hours, and now I got fourteen hours a day, everyday. Ninety per cent of my crimes were committed late in the night, and now I have a worker with me every night. So I am never alone.' April spoke about her dependency on 'support staff' and the lack of attention paid to her desire to employ female-only staff in her home: 'I don't like to stay alone, so I guess I will always need respite workers. I wouldn't want men [as respite workers], but you got no choice.' Jennifer is a recipient of the assertive case management approach and requires constant monitoring in her life, in large part because of her psychiatric illness. She explained:

> I have five different home care workers. I had a meeting yesterday, and every week workers are given an opportunity to go to a meeting and discuss problems and concerns they are having. The only thing I got against me now is that I use the phone once too often [laughs]. So if that's going to be the worst thing, then I think I am going to do okay. I mean, I know there are going to be times when I am possibly going to have to go back to the hospital for a couple of days or whatever, but the other part is I have a good doctor now, and when I go in to see him he doesn't just spend five minutes with me and then that's it. I will spend an hour or so with him. I also have a case manager, which is something that I have never had.

Reliance on home-care staff to control many aspects of women's lives is clearly evidenced by Jennifer, who talked about practical issues of money management:

> I didn't have any security. I would go home at night and pass out on the floor and probably have a cigarette burn or something like that. Wake up the next morning, not even the next morning but a few hours later awakened by someone banging on my door because the house was full of smoke. I mean I even actually almost destroyed the house that my parents built in 1983. I think, too, now I was the one who decided that I didn't want my cheques coming in my name or to my address, so the way we got it worked out is on cheque days my cheque would go to Emmanuel House, and my worker would come and pick me up here and we would go up and do the things we have to do.

The continuum of control in the lives of criminalized women has been well established in this study. Women's pathways into prison are typically marked by layers of social control that can begin at a very young age. Quite apart from the criminal justice system, the myriad of state control forces in women's lives continue to play a major role in their lives after they leave prison. State-sponsored control forces continue to be present in women's lives long after their sentences have expired. For the most part, the women who have successfully stayed out of trouble and therefore have not landed themselves back in prison are now equally controlled by locally run agents. Again, this finding is not new. It has been the subject of much previous scholarship. The extended intrusion into the so-called private lives of women ex-prisoners has now been taken up by local agencies who receive their core funding from government sponsors and who are expected to do more, with less.

The local penal industrial complex has largely escaped the scrutiny of prison abolitionists and other radicals who rightly point to the economic development opportunities provided by prisons. Through no real fault of these well-intentioned local organizations, we are now witnessing the enormous costs associated with institutional maintenance being downloaded onto local groups who have inadequate resources to effectively target the needs of women ex-prisoners. This is certainly the case with government per diem contributions to local groups operating residential centres for parolees.

In addition to home supports and ongoing intrusions by state officials (e.g., welfare and child protection) many women on coming out of prison are required, as a condition of release, to reside at a halfway house. The absence of women-only accommodations in the Atlantic region requires that women parolees accept space at a residential centre in the province's capital that primarily houses male sex offenders and former psychiatric patients. This practice is in stark contrast to the woman-centred approach the Correctional Service of Canada purports to have. While the use of such language has gained considerable prominence in the everyday vocabulary of governments, it is ill-defined and lacks consensual meaning. In penal discourse, the term *woman-centred* is supposedly the guiding philosophy behind institutional and local initiatives in Canada. It has been repeatedly pointed out that such an approach has failed in prisons, and the application of this philosophy has not even been contemplated outside them. It has already been argued that the basic principles of woman-centredness are incongruent with the penal goals of punishment and surveillance that operate simultaneously on the outside. A number of concerns arise from this definition and its specific application to local initiatives for women. As Hannah-Moffat has argued, this approach is problematic from the start: 'Current regimes and proposed visions of woman-centered corrections often fail to depart from traditional conceptualizations of punishment. The definition and constitution of a woman-centered regime is troublesome for the following reasons: It relies on the problematic category of "woman"; it is insensitive to wider social, economic, political, and cultural relations of power; it sets up a false dichotomy between the woman-centered and the male-centered regimes; and it denies the legal and material realities of imprisonment. Further ... [w]oman-centered reforms rely on a flexible rationality of empowerment. The language of empowerment is used to legitimate both correctional and feminist strategies. The difficulty is that reformers and the state are working with different interpretations of empowerment' (1995: 36).

Hannah-Moffat rightly contends that feminists have failed to address the meaning and criteria of woman-centredness and the implementation of the task force's recommendations. As a result, the definition of woman-centredness has been left to Corrections Canada with little external feminist input. Many of the above-noted issues become even more problematic in terms of locally run programs, that are paid for by the state but are not held accountable for upholding the guiding principles of such an approach. Therefore, what we are witnessing on the outside in terms of housing and treatment programs is a reversion to a male-centred model, based largely on numbers and economics, to the detriment of women. One very distressing example of the consequences is the practice of requiring women parolees to reside in residential facilities with male sex offenders, which does nothing to further the women's attempts at rehabilitation.

Attendance at mandatory group counselling sessions for women on the outside also raises a number of pressing concerns with regard to confidentiality and opening up about past abuses in a group in which there are male sex offenders. Clearly, a multi-purpose approach to treatment and programming that takes men as the common denominator in program design and delivery tends to replicate the very same problems cited previously. Again, a lack of accountability means that the goal of empowering women has been lost. An emphasis on empowering women is another purported component of Canada's penal philosophy, but, once more, this term is problematic and open to a wide range of subjective interpretations by the government, feminists, and criminalized women themselves. As Pollack has argued, 'most models of empower-

ment prioritize an individualistic or psychological notion of empowerment, thereby minimizing the importance of social influences and
oppression ... [I]ndividualizing social issues can result in blaming individuals for problems that arise from being oppressed in various ways
and may be further disempowering to them' (2000: 76). Cognitive-based
treatment and assertive case management approaches such as those
adopted in terms of mandatory treatment programs for women psychologize and individualize women's empowerment. Tensions cannot help
but arise when a system attempts at the same time both to control and
to empower women in a coercive penal environment now set up in local
neighbourhoods.

Conclusion: Where to From Here?

While the term [community] may appeal to a warm, nostalgic sense of 'belonging' among the self-proclaimed law-abiding, its promise of inclusivity can be interpreted in contradictory ways when applied to those who break the law and are criminalised. Far from demonstrating that it is resourceful, tolerant, and healing, the community is then rejecting, excluding and intolerantly punitive.

Worrall 1997: 47

This book confirms several well-known pathways to women's criminalization including poverty, sexual and physical abuse, histories of state controls, and defiance of gender norms. Moreover, it reveals several important new findings. First, the more layers of social control that a woman has encountered throughout her life, the less likely it is that she will stay out of prison. These layers of social control include foster care, child protection, prolonged reliance on social assistance, and interactions with psychiatry and/or mental health agencies. State-sponsored controls, often under the guise of local agents, continue to pervade women's lives long after their sentences have expired.

Second, success and/or failure are very subjective categories in people's lives and do not coincide with official definitions. As a penal management tool, recidivism rates are an unreliable indicator of women's overall performance and functionality outside prisons. These statistical scales tell us nothing about how women are managing their everyday lives. These measures do a further injustice by labelling individuals according to a numeric scale that camouflages many issues women face upon returning to their communities (such as inadequate housing, poverty, and abuse) and reflect neoliberal ideologies that place blame for 'failing to make it' on individual women.

Third, among the group of women who have stayed out of the prison system, an overwhelming number have significant mental illnesses and, therefore, are now confined in a psychiatric hospital or in their own homes with full-time 'respite' workers. Patterns of dependency, medicalization, and infantilization persist in the treatment of women at the local level. The penal industrial complex is clearly evidenced throughout this book. Not surprisingly, given the limited financial resources available to local organizations, non-profit groups are scrambling over the finite allotment of money for delivery of social services. This results in local organizations attempting to operate under a multi-purpose banner by offering themselves as candidates for several pockets of government funding. Local agencies reliant on core government funding are now expected to be everything to everyone. For the state, this means doing business at a cut rate with non-profit agencies and without interference. For the non-profit organizations, surveillance now takes precedence over advocacy. For women who have been in prison, this means a replication of control and a diminished trust in local agency staff who double as counsellors and enforcers.

Finally, although well-known factors such as safe and affordable housing, meaningful employment, and supportive relationships are cited as key contributors to women's staying out, they are not enough in and of themselves to keep women out of prison. Safe and adequate housing and meaningful employment should be a guarantee for all women in a country as rich as Canada and should not be a risk marker that sets women up for further 'failure.' Transcarceral patterns of social control are clearly in evidence throughout this book, and often their roots go back long before a woman is sentenced to prison. Incarceration in a penal institution represents another stepping stone along the continuum of formal social controls in the lives of many such women. Shuffling from one institution to another throughout their entire lives, prison all too often represents the juncture at which 'help,' albeit quite minimal help, is found. Notwithstanding this sad reality, leaving prison in no way marks the end of a woman's period of incarceration. Although much has been written about transcarceration and social control, placing gender at the forefront of such investigations is a critical exercise. Women are much more vulnerable than are men to controls based on societal conceptions of family and motherhood and the prescribed roles of men and women. Women continue to be penalized for transgressing traditional sex roles, and they are often subjected to controls that favour medicalized conformity.

Policy Directions

There is no shortage of policy recommendations that can be generated from this study. It is important to recognize, however, that policy proposals aimed specifically at reforming the criminal (in)justice system amount to little more than tinkering with one part of a much wider system that is failing women. A critical assessment of the broader capitalist patriarchal structures that characterize and subvert the lives of Canadian women more generally is needed. However, in recognizing that an overthrow of capitalist patriarchal structures will not take place overnight, we have to be vigilant in the meantime and correct the systemically based inequalities that operate at every level of our society to further marginalize and disempower criminalized women. In keeping with the findings of this research and the call for a transgressive criminology, policy suggestions aimed at reforming Canada's criminal (in)justice system are largely averted in favour of broader systemic reforms that extend outside the confines of the prison.

Undoubtedly, the key policy proposal advanced here is an ideological one. As DeKeseredy and colleagues have made clear, 'ideological hurdles rather than economic obstacles account for the failure to mount rational campaigns to bring about social justice' (2003: 125). Therefore, a much broader platform of social justice needs to be adopted in dealing with criminalized women given the myriad factors that converge to further disadvantage this particular group.

The feminization and subsequent criminalization of poverty are ever-increasing in Canada. Given that the overwhelming majority of women's crimes are survival crimes, issues surrounding women's increasing poverty and economic marginalization need to be more closely addressed from the perspectives of the conditions that propel women 'into conflict with the law' in the first place, while also assessing the role of women's economic marginalization in direct relation to their chances of successful completion of their parole terms. Underlying the narratives of women's pathways into prison and their continued struggle to stay out is the failure of welfare policies to provide a decent living income. As Mosher and colleagues have reminded us, 'what is needed most urgently and most profoundly is a fundamental paradigm shift; a shift from viewing poverty as the failing of individuals, and those who are lazy, unmotivated and deceptive. To the extent that the welfare system ... continues to operate from such a paradigm, there is really little hope that it will offer meaningful support to facilitate women's safe exit from abusive relationships. Women will continue to be subjected to demeaning, humiliating treatment; will be constantly regarded with suspicion; and will be subject to the control and discipline of the state' (2004: vi).

Turning back to the case of Kimberly Rogers (discussed in Chapter 3), we know that poverty kills. The draconian policies that were in place at the time of Ms Rogers death are still in place – and have actually worsened. Kimberly Rogers was caught in the cruel web of social assistance policies that are obviously inadequate. Dramatic cuts to benefits, the repeal of discretionary benefits for pregnant women, mandatory workfare, increased vigilance in monitoring, and the lifetime ban for anyone convicted of welfare fraud are designed to make it harder for people like Kimberly Rogers to 'get by' on social assistance. A campaign established in response to the death of Kimberly Rogers noted that 'social assistance policy in Ontario needs a major overhaul to meet the needs of poor people. The Province must first set benefits at adequate levels; increase funds for training and employment to pre-1995 levels (adjusted for cost of living); allow social assistance recipients to receive both assistance benefits and student loans; repeal the lifetime ban on collecting social assistance benefits after a welfare fraud conviction; make it easier for people in need to qualify for social assistance and stop violating Canada's human rights commitments and international treaty obligations' (DisAbled Women's Network Ontario undated).

Before her death, Kimberly Rogers became the first Ontario citizen to launch a case under Canada's Charter of Rights and Freedoms that challenged the constitutional validity of Ontario Works regulations that suspended her benefits. Her Charter case argued on several grounds, including: (1) the law that allowed welfare authorities to disqualify her from receiving assistance contravenes the Charter rights to life, liberty, and security of the person; (2) cutting off her assistance after she had already been severely punished constituted 'cruel and unusual punishment'; and (3) as a pregnant woman with a diagnosed disability, the automatic suspension infringed the Charter's guarantee of equality. In making her decision, the judge pointed to Canada's human rights commitments and stated: 'In the unique circumstances of this case, if [Ms Rogers] is exposed to the full three months' suspension of her benefits, a member of our community carrying an unborn child may well be homeless and deprived of basic sustenance. Such a situation would jeopardize the health of Ms Rogers and the fetus, thereby adversely affecting not only mother and child but also the public – its dignity, its human rights commitments and its health care resources' (Justice Epstein, Ontario Superior Court of Justice, 31 May 2001).

Following Kimberly Rogers' lead, we need to seek legal redress mechanisms that guarantee our rights under the Charter. Freedom from discrimination based on economic disadvantage should be enshrined in our fundamental rights. Coalitions of women's equality-seeking groups, such as the campaign that brought about the systemic review of women's prisons, are a step in the right direction. Building alliances to target the Charter of Human Rights and Freedoms as a redress mechanism for enforcing Canada's constitutional obligations to women is one progressive means of achieving equality (Jhappan 2002).

For academics, a trangressive criminology that starts from outside criminological discourse is advocated. Feminist criminologists 'must explore the total lives of women, and there are no tools in existing crim-inological theory with which to do this' (Cain 1990: 10). Furthermore, 'it simply has not proved possible to make adequate sense of what is going on in these areas of concern by starting from inside criminologi-cal discourse. Only by starting from outside, with the social construc-tion of gender, or with women's experiences of their total lives, or with the structure of the domestic space, can we begin to make sense of what is going on' (ibid.).

Criminalized women are among the most marginalized in our society. These women are being increasingly marginalized and subsequently regulated at every turn based on their increasing poverty; their roles as primary caregivers; their histories of physical and sexual abuse that result in a double victimization of women by the state; the layers of for-mal social controls that characterize criminalized women's lives; the increasing criminalization of mental illness; and their resistance to patri-archal gender norms that is being increasingly met with punishment. In theorizing the criminalization of women, I am continually drawn back to the work of transgressive criminology because I fail to see what crim-inology in and of itself can offer to the lives of these women. Outside of tinkering with the correctional machinery, the real issues affecting the lives of criminalized women in a capitalist patriarchy are left unat-tended. Feminist criminology still exists as an adjunct to the established body of 'malestream' criminological knowledge (e.g., 'add women and stir approach'). The study of crime continues to be shaped by men's experiences and exalts men as the standard by which research and the-ory are constructed. Women are seen as Other, when they are taken into account at all. Moving outside criminology, then, forces a shift in focus towards the broader fundamentals of feminist thought and a critical analysis of the traditional and contemporary assumptions of criminology as an androcentric discipline that fails to take gender seriously by placing it at the periphery of inquiry and analysis.

Starting from a socialist feminist stance, we view women's life experiences as shaped by both class and gender. Patriarchy, thus, is the driving force behind women's oppression, and it is continually reproduced and reinforced through such institutions as marriage, child-rearing, and sexual practices. Strategies for change rest on the overthrow of patriarchal relations, which would permit women's sexual autonomy and obliterate the oppressive nature of sexual and familial relations for women. This broader feminist approach moves us away from a preoccupation with the corrections system to more fundamental issues affecting the lives of all women. It leads us to critically focus on the penal industrial complex that has supported a dramatic drop in welfare and education to fund the prison endeavour. Resources that were once used to support low-income women and their children and to enhance education efforts have been reallocated to the ever-expanding penal (and military) enterprise. We need to look to the erosion of our social safety net under a neoliberal government strategy that predominantly targets women and drives them further into poverty and despair, rather than narrowing our focus to those women who get caught up in the machinery of the criminal justice system. We also need to be very critical of the increasing medicalization of certain disadvantaged groups (Conrad and Schneider 1985).

As evidenced in this book, women's trajectories into and out of prison are marked by often long-standing patterns of poverty, abuse, addictions, histories of formal social controls, and defiance of gender role norms. These factors converge in ways that are clearly non-linear. That is, these conditions overlap with one another to produce a lifestyle of (unwanted) dependencies on the state. In turn, these dependencies become further entrenched in a criminal justice system that fosters a culture of dependency and does nothing to contribute to women's economic and social empowerment. The compounding effects of incarceration on the lives of women who have, for the most part, been excluded by society on the basis of their class, gender, sexuality, and cultural differences, need to be the core focus of any reintegration efforts on their behalf whether made by the state or by local organizations. We have been vigilant in our efforts to expose the human rights violations in prisons. The same critical appraisal needs to be made of the outside, where the social regulation of women begins and ends. As academics and activists, we need to be very critical of punishment in the community, because 'there is nothing in the appeal to community which offers any fundamental criticism of oppressive traditional sexual divisions of labour or social practices of racial intolerance and exclusion' (Worrall 1997: 48). The reality is that communities are also fractured along divisions of age, race and gender.

To go full circle and back to my initial positioning and reflection on the lives of the women who are the real voices of this work and who once sat as my young friends in an elementary school classroom, I am reminded of the quotation often cited by Kim Pate, one of the leading international activists on behalf of criminalized women in Canada:

> If you have come here to help [or study] me,
> you are wasting your time,
> If you have come here because
> your liberation is bound up with mine,
> then let us work together. (2003: 169)

These words epitomize my heart-felt position that the voices of women in this book cannot be neatly separated by their formal process of criminalization. There is a shadow line between the direction in which their lives have gone and the direction in which they might otherwise have headed had it not been for the layering of structural and gendered inequalities that precipitate and continue to exacerbate their encounters with Canada's criminal (in)justice system. Achieving equality is a struggle that we are all in together. Until every woman has achieved substantive equality, none of us can claim victory.

Appendix: Research Guide

Can we begin with a few background questions?
1. How old are you?
2. What is your present marital status?
3. How much schooling have you completed?
4. Are you currently employed?
   If yes, what type of work do you do?
   What type of work have you done in the past?
   Probe: Employment history, level of training, nature of employment (full-time, part-time, seasonal), job satisfaction, future employment plans, future education/training plans.
5. What is your major source of income? (social assistance, Employment Insurance, Disability Insurance, full or part-time employment, other)

Can we now talk a little now about your criminal history and prison experiences?
6. Can you give me a sketch of your past criminal convictions?
   Probe: Juvenile record, types and length of convictions, federal/provincial incarceration.
7. Can you describe your prison experiences?
8. Were you involved in programming at the prison? If so, what type, length, nature, etc?
9. Would you say that your prison experience equipped you to cope with your eventual release?
   Probe: Release plans.
10. What sorts of problems/difficulties, if any, did prison present for you in terms of being released? For your family? For your children?
    Probe: Pains of Imprisonment

Now can we turn to your community release experiences?

11. What type of community release were you granted?
    Probe: Statutory release, probation order, mandatory release.
12. What portion of your sentence was served in the community?
13. What conditions were placed upon your release?
    Probe: Halfway house, counselling, employment training, reporting to a probation/parole officer.
14. Can you describe your experiences in going from prison into the community?
    Probe: Transitional period from prison back into the community.

Another important area in discussing your prison and community experiences might be child care responsibilities.

15. Do you have children? If so, what are their ages?
16. Do they live with you? (Living arrangements before incarceration and during community sentence.)
17. With whom did they live during your incarceration?
18. How would you say being on community sentence affected your day-to-day interactions with your kids, if at all?
    Probe: What impact did incarceration and community release have on your children? Attendance at programming? Visits to parole office?

Can we talk now about your experiences after prison?

19. Can you describe the different agencies you were involved with during probation (e.g., mental health, child protection, welfare, etc.)?
20. Did you participate in programming upon your release? If so, describe the nature and frequency of these sessions? Did you find these programs useful?
    Probe: Who/what constituted the 'community' for these women?
21. Where were these programs offered? By whom?
22. Can you describe any barriers/challenges you faced in community reintegration and how you managed to deal with these obstacles?
    Probe: Gender-specific programming.
23. What supports were made available to you during your community term?
    Probe: Employment counselling, child care, mandatory programming, etc.
24. What role(s) did community organizations play in your staying out / returning?

Probe: Community mental health services, programs/treatment services, familial/peer supports, community education resources, Social Services, Correctional Service Canada, Department of Justice, Child Protection Services, and non-profit service agencies.

25. What do you see as the major needs of women being released to the community?
    Probe: Housing, child care, employment, peer support, counselling / mental health services.

26. Are these needs being met? If so, how? Explain.
    If not, how could they be met?

27. What would you describe as the major factors which contributed to the successful (or unsuccessful) completion of your community sentence?

28. What would it take to keep you from coming back to prison? Alternatively, what would bring you back into prison?

Thank you so much for your time and patience in completing this interview.

Notes

Introduction

1 The 'corrective' nature of the competing goals of incarceration (e.g., punishment vs rehabilitation) is challenged throughout this research. As Horii (2000: 107) has argued, 'corrections is plainly a misnomer since reformatories, lockups, jails, prisons and penitentiaries correct nothing, rather they err.'

2 The concept of 'woman-centredness' is challenged throughout this book. Despite its original intentions, it has amounted to little more than a misappropriation of feminist goodwill and as such serves a further injustice to criminalized women.

3 Empowering women in the most disempowering of environments such as the prison has been debated by feminist scholars (e.g., Hannah-Moffat 2000; Pollack 2000).

4 The term *incarcerated* refers to physical incapacitation in a prison. It is understood, however, that incarceration takes many forms, and women are as easily incapacitated in their homes and communities under various forms of state controls. Electronic monitoring and house arrest are also forms of incarceration (see Maidment 2002).

5 A critical investigation of what constitutes the *community* for this group of sentenced women in Newfoundland and Labrador is a major focus of my 'Research Guide' (see Appendix). However, it is critical that the women themselves were given the opportunity to define what the community means for them.

6 A singular, quantifiable definition of *success* is not proffered in my research. However, according to Correctional Services Canada (CSC) definitions, recidivism rates are the official barometer of success and are defined as

'any new conviction for an offence committed within two years of release from prison' (see Bonta, Rugge, and Dauvergne 2003; Bonta, Pang, and Wallace-Carpretta 1995). This definition is problematic for a number of reasons which are explored throughout this book.

7 The term *reintegration* is problematized here for many of the same reasons discussed in the problematizing of language. It is based on classist, racist, and sexist ideals of how one should behave.

8 The term *prisoning* is adopted from Comack (1996: 124) and refers to 'the *process* of incarceration/imprisonment and ... plac[ing] the focus on women's experiences of that process.'

9 In the determination of an individual's risk level, CSC relies upon the integration of both legal and dynamic factors. Legal factors, for example, include one's length of sentence, severity of the offence, and any history of violence. Dynamic factors include one's willingness to comply, attitude, criminal associations, and evidence of any substance abuse. Demographic factors such as age, education, and employment are also factored into determining risk levels.

10 The major criterion for my sample was four or more prison admissions over an eleven-year period. Because the majority of imprisoned women are serving a first-time sentence, I did not want to capture that group of women who may have had a one-time, isolated run-in with the criminal justice system and then 'naturally' migrated away from the prison system. My target group is those women for whom prison has played a significant role throughout their adult lives. This selection of four prior admissions yielded a sample size of twenty-four.

11 Although this research does not make initial claims as to the definition of *success* or *failure*, it was determined at the sampling stage to impose the two-year non-custodial cut-off as a measure in keeping with the official definitions of recidivism for sampling purposes only. However, imposing this two-year period raised important concerns and questions regarding the reliability and validity of this measurement tool. For example, staying out of prison past two years did not necessarily translate into being offence-free during this same time.

12 It is extremely difficult to try and locate the factors that contribute to conformity (in the legal sense) and subsequent non-criminalization. Indeed, this is an undertaking that would undoubtedly produce inconclusive results as attempts to isolate dependent from independent variables would vary widely. For example, the weighting of different variables (e.g., work ethic, family support, role modelling, and (in)formal education) would prove extremely problematic to quantify, disentangle, and prioritize.

13 Many of us, for a variety of reasons, escape the formal criminalization process (i.e., arrest and sentencing), particularly as young persons, despite the commission of criminal activities. This is certainly an important area of investigation in and of itself.

14 The Canadian Association of Elizabeth Fry Societies (CAEFS) is an 'association of self-governing, community-based Elizabeth Fry Societies that work with and for women and girls in the justice system, particularly those who are, or may be, criminalized. Together, Elizabeth Fry Societies develop and advocate the beliefs, principles and positions that guide CAEFS. The association exists to ensure substantive equality in the delivery and development of services and programs through public education, research, legislative and administrative reform, regionally, nationally and internationally' (CAEFS, Mission Statement). In Canada, there are twenty-five local Elizabeth Fry societies. For more information on the workings of this organization, see http://www.elizabethfry.ca/caefs_e.htm.

Chapter 1

1 It has been argued that any criminal justice system does not serve justice for all or in all circumstances. For example, it has been consistently well documented that the poor are discriminated against at every stage of the criminal justice system (see, e.g., Merton 1938; Cohen 1955; Cloward and Ohlin 1960; Quinney 1970; Carlen 1988; Young 1999; Reiman 2004). Others show that the same holds true for women (e.g., Faith 1993), First Nations people (e.g., Nielsen and Silverman 1996), and minorities (e.g., Mann 1993).

2 While I acknowledge the necessity of serious interrogations of the language used to describe women's criminal involvement, it is beyond the scope of this study to deal sufficiently with each of these issues. It is brought to the reader's attention in order to raise sensitivity to the importance of language and related gendered power structures that further oppress women.

3 NIMBY (Not in My Backyard) is a common resistance strategy used by neighbourhood associations to protest the location in their areas of halfway houses and other 'undesirables.'

4 Socialist feminism still focuses largely on gender and class and does not adequately address race as a contributing factor to women's oppression.

5 Smith (1987: 107–9) argues that women's lives have been outside of or subordinate to the relations of ruling. However, she also argues, that it is not only women who are excluded. The ruling apparatus is 'an organization of class and as such implicates dominant classes. It also excludes the many voices of women and men of colour, native peoples, and gays and lesbians.

From different standpoints different aspects of the ruling apparatus and of class come into view.'

6 I reject the language that pathologizes women and therefore do not use 'cognitive disabilities,' which infers 'faulty thinking patterns.'

7 For an elaborate discussion of the parallels between slavery and prison, see Angela Davis, 'Slavery, Civil Rights, and Abolitionist Perspectives toward Prison,' in *Are Prisons Obsolete?* (2003).

8 Local (community) controls include day parole, full parole, or statutory release, as well as controls on those who are temporarily detained or paroled for deportation (Canada, Solicitor General 2002).

9 This refers to prisoners being classified as high risk, which does not accurately reflect their crimes or the so-called threat that they pose to society. It is the conflation of 'risk' and 'need' that contributes to women's overclassification. A much higher percentage of women tend to be classified as requiring maximum security compared with their male counterparts (Hannah-Moffat and Shaw 2003).

10 An example of this legitimation process by the state is the inclusion of 'control talk' (Cohen 1985) that replaced the language used to describe the work of front-line prison workers, formerly known as guards or correctional officers, with the supposed gender sensitivity of a reclassification wherein staff are now known as 'primary care workers.'

11 *Creating Choices* outlined a model of woman-centredness based on these five guiding principles. For a more in-depth discussion of the shortcomings and limitations of this approach within a custodial setting, see Hannah-Moffat and Shaw 2000.

12 Correctional personnel or systemic net-widening focuses on the added costs associated with social network expansion, specifically in the form of additional personnel and program service delivery (Mainprize 1992).

13 Offender net-widening refers to bringing more offenders into the correctional system who would otherwise be eligible for less intrusive 'alternative' sanctions, such as probation and parole (Mainprize 1992).

14 These costs do not include annual operating budgets, nor do they account for the costs associated with the warehousing of federally sentenced women within men's prisons.

Chapter 2

1 Statistics Canada determines whether a family is low-income by 'comparing the income of an economic family to a low-income cutoff (LICO), which varies according to family size and the size of the area of residence. The

LICO values are chosen by estimating at what income families spend 20 percentage points more than average on food, shelter and clothing' (Canada, Statistics Canada 2002).

2 The distance from St John's, Newfoundland, where a majority of federally sentenced women and their families reside, to Truro, Nova Scotia, is 1,315 kilometres.

3 Truro is a small town in Nova Scotia with little in the way of infrastructure to serve the needs of women prisoners. The larger centre of Halifax would have provided much more access to resources, as well as facilitating family visits, given the centrality of its location in Atlantic Canada.

4 On 8 March 2001, International Women's Day, the Canadian Association of Elizabeth Fry Societies (CAEFS), in conjunction with the Native Women's Association of Canada (NWAC) urged a broad-based systemic review, pursuant to section 61(2) of the Canadian Human Rights Act, regarding the treatment of federally sentenced women. As part of the process of developing submissions to the Canadian Human Rights Commission (CHRC), CAEFS consulted with twenty-seven other national women's, Aboriginal, and justice groups. The CHRC circulated a discussion paper to individual and organizational stakeholders who work on behalf of federally sentenced women. In May 2003, the coalition of equality-seeking groups each made submissions to the CHRC based on this report.

Chapter 3

1 The Corrections and Community Services Branch, Department of Justice, release their divisional reports on a bi-annual basis; however, the most recent statistical report used (2000–1) does not contain custodial breakdowns based on sex (Newfoundland and Labrador, Department of Justice 2001).

2 Federal-provincial Exchange of Service Agreements (ESA) allow some federal prisoners to serve their sentences in their home province. ESAs contribute significantly to a province's penal budget. For example, in 2000–1, Newfoundland and Labrador was reimbursed by the federal government $3,114,700 for the detention of federal prisoners (both males and females; ibid.).

3 The National Parole Board (NPB) has jurisdiction in all provinces except Ontario, Quebec, and British Columbia, where provincial parole boards have been established. Provincial and territorial governments are responsible for all other services, including custodial sentences of less than two years, remand of prisoners, other forms of temporary detention (e.g., immi-

gration holds), and localized punishment (probation, electronic monitoring, conditional sentencing) (Canadian Centre for Justice Statistics 2002). Probation and conditional sentencing are court-ordered and supervised locally, while parole and statutory release are part of a custodial sentence.

4 Based on the work of Memorial University sociologist Dr Larry Felt, this database was made available to me for my research.

5 Four admissions was taken as the point at which there appeared to be a natural break between prisoners who have experienced few sentences and those who are repeatedly criminalized. The majority of women in my sample had a considerably higher number of prison admissions.

6 Of the total contacted, two women refused participation; one was unavailable for interview because she now resides permanently in a psychiatric hospital; three could not be located in the province; and seven had moved outside the province of Newfoundland and Labrador. Given the budget of this study, I was not in a position to travel to other Canadian centres to conduct interviews. The experiences of the criminalized women who move away in search of employment opportunities would certainly have enriched the study results had this been possible.

7 I fully intend at a later time to compare my manually generated output with results generated using a qualitative computer package. I am interested in contrasting the results according to the respective methods, and therefore provide further insight into the processes of knowledge production and legitimation.

Chapter 4

1 The ethnic breakdown of the total sample is as follows: Inuit (7%), Innu (0.9%), Métis (0.3%), African American (0.3%), of European descent (89.6%), Other (2%).

2 The Waterford is the primary psychiatric hospital located in St John's, and it 'offers acute, rehabilitative and continuing care to those 16 and older with mental health problems and mental illnesses.' This historic hospital located on Waterford Bridge Road was first opened in 1854 as the Hospital for Mental and Nervous Diseases. It was renamed the Waterford Hospital in 1972.

3 A recent epidemic of OxyContin abuse in Newfoundland resulted in the creation of a provincial task force to 'identify the nature and extent of the problem related to OxyContin abuse and ... [m]ake recommendations to limit unauthorized access and inappropriate use of OxyContin and other related narcotics' (Newfoundland and Labrador, Department of Health,

May 2004). OxyContin is a prescription drug often used in management of acute pain in cancer patients. Because of its controlled-release property, OxyContin contains more oxycodone and needs to be taken less often than other oxycodone-containing drugs. This feature of the drug has led to a 400 per cent increase in the quantity of OxyContin tablets prescribed in the province from 2000 to 2003 (ibid.).

4 Recently, a 'restraint chair' has been brought into the NLCCW as a means of confining women who 'act out.' Needless to say, the introduction of this controlling technique is an illustration of the barbaric and draconian measures practised in many provincial (and federal) prisons.

5 The Newfoundland and Labrador Youth Centre (NLYC), located in Whitbourne (78 kilometres outside St John's), was operationalized in 1992. The NLYC has been deemed the primary secure custody centre for youth in the province. It is a sixty-bed institution and accommodates young persons sentenced to secure custody, as well as those remanded for psychiatric assessment, trial, or sentencing (Newfoundland and Labrador, Department of Justice 2001).

6 This shocking autobiography of a foster child uncovers abuses by the Roman Catholic church in the delivery of foster 'care' services; Derek O'Brien, its author, is a former resident of Mount Cashel Orphanage in St John's (O'Brien 1991).

7 The ten-bed Pleasantville Youth Centre is the only other secure custody centre in the province, besides Whitbourne. It primarily serves the greater St John's Census Metropolitan Area (CMA) and incarcerates young persons who have been temporarily detained by the police, are on short-term remands, or are awaiting psychiatric assessments.

Chapter 5

1 Canadian 'corrections' is operated on a two-tiered system: federal sentences are managed by the Correctional Services of Canada (CSC) and include sentences of two years or more. The federal government also has responsibility for statutory release and parole supervision. See also chapter 3, n2.

2 Her Majesty's Penitentiary (HMP) is a medium security men's prison located in St John's.

3 MHA is the acronym used to describe those detained in prison under the provincial Mental Health Act.

4 Stoplifters is a shoplifting intervention program operated by several provincial Elizabeth Fry Societies across Canada.

References

Abell, J. 2001. *Structural Adjustment and the New Poor Laws: Gender, Poverty and Violence and Canada's International Commitments*. Ottawa: Canadian Feminist Alliance for International Action.

Adelberg, E., and Currie, C. (eds.). 1993. *In Conflict with the Law: Women and the Canadian Justice System*. Vancouver: Press Gang Publishers.

Adler, F. 1975. *Sisters in Crime: The Rise of the New Female Criminal*. New York: McGraw-Hill.

Andersen, M. 2003. *Thinking about Women: Sociological Perspectives on Sex and Gender*. Needham Heights: Allyn and Bacon.

Andrews, D. 1989. 'Recidivism Is Predictable and Can Be Influenced: Using Risk Assessments to Reduce Recidivism.' *Forum on Corrections Research* 1(2): 11–18.

Andrews, D., and Bonta, J. 1998. *The Psychology of Criminal Conduct*. Cincinnati: Anderson.

Arbour, L. 1996. *Commission of Inquiry into Certain Events at the Prison for Women in Kingston*. Ottawa: Public Works and Government Services Canada.

Becker, H. 1963. *Outsiders*. New York: Free Press.

Beckett, K., and Western, B. 2001. 'Governing Social Marginality: Welfare, Incarceration, and the Transformation of State Policy.' In *Mass Imprisonment: Social Causes and Consequences*, ed. D. Garland, 35–50. London: Sage.

Bertrand, M.-A. 1979. *La femme et le crime*. Montreal: Éditions l'Aurore.

Bertrand, M.-A., Biron, L., Di Pisa, C., Fagnan, A., and McLean, J. 1998. *Prisons pour femmes*. Montreal: Éditions du Méridien.

Berzins, L., and Colette-Carrière, R. 1979. 'Les femmes en prison: Un inconvénient social!' *Santé mentale au Québec* 4(2): 87–103.

Blanchette, K. 1997. *Risk and Need among Federally-Sentenced Female Offenders: A Comparison of Minimum, Medium, and Maximum Security Inmates*. Research Report R-58. Ottawa: Correctional Service Canada.

Blomberg, T. 2003. 'Penal Reforms and the Fate of Alternatives.' In *Punishment and Social Control*, ed. T. Blomberg and S. Cohen, 417–31. New York: Aldine de Gruyter.

Bonta, J., Pang, B., and Wallace-Capretta, S. 1995. 'Predictors of Recidivism among Incarcerated Female Offenders.' *Prison Journal* 75(3): 277–94.

Bonta, J., Rugge, T., and Dauvergne, M. 2003. *The Reconviction Rate of Female Offenders*. User Report 2003–02. Ottawa: Solicitor General Canada.

Boritch, H. 1997. *Female Crime and Criminal Justice in Canada*. Toronto: ITP Nelson.

Burke, A. 2002. 'Triple Jeopardy: Women Marginalized by Substance Abuse, Poverty, and Incarceration.' In *Women at the Margins: Neglect, Punishment, and Resistance*, ed. J. Figueira-McDonough and R. Sarri, 175–201. London: Haworth Press.

Burstyn, V. 1983. 'Masculine Dominance and the State.' In *The Socialist Register*, ed. R. Miliband, and J. Saville, 45–89. London: Merlin Press.

Cain, M. 1990. 'Towards Transgression: New Directions in Feminist Criminology.' *International Journal of the Sociology of Law* 18: 1–18.

Callaghan, M., Farha, L., and Porter, B. 2002. *Women and Housing in Canada: Barriers to Equality*. Toronto: Women's Housing Program, Centre for Equality Rights and Accommodation.

Canada, Auditor General. 2003. Report of the Auditor General of Canada, Chapter 4: 'Reintegration of Women Offenders.' Available at http://oag-bvg.gc.ca/domino/reports.nsf/html/200304ce.html.

Canada, House of Commons, Standing Committee on Public Accounts. 2003. *Twenty-sixth Report of the Standing Committee on Public Accounts. Chapter 4 of the April 2003 Report of the Auditor General of Canada – Correctional Service of Canada – Reintegration of Women Offenders*. Ottawa: Public Works and Government Services. Available at http://www.parl.gc.ca/infoCom/PubDocument.asp.

Canada, Solicitor General. 2002. *Corrections and Conditional Release Statistical Overview*. Ottawa: author.

– 2001. *Women in Canada*. Canadian Centre for Justice Statistics Profile Series. Ottawa: author.

– 2002. *Low Income Cutoffs from 1992 to 2001 and Low Income Measures from 1991 to 2000*. Ottawa: author.

Canadian Association of Elizabeth Fry Societies. 2005. *Facts Sheets*. Ottawa: author.

– 2003a. *Submission of the Canadian Association of Elizabeth Fry Societies (CAEFS) to the Canadian Human Rights Commission for the Special Report on the Discrimi-*

nation on the Basis of Sex, Race and Disability Faced by Federally Sentenced Women. Ottawa: author.

– 2003b. *CAEFS's Response to the Discussion Paper of the Canadian Human Rights Commission.* Ottawa: author.

Canadian Broadcasting Corporation. 2004. *Paid to Be Poor.* CBC Radio One. Available at http://www.cbc.ca/paidtobepoor/

Canadian Centre for Justice Statistics. 2005. *Adult Correctional Services in Canada, 2003/04.* Ottawa: Statistics Canada.

– 2002. *Adult Correctional Services in Canada, 2000/01.* Ottawa: Statistics Canada.

Canadian Council on Social Development. 2005. *Poverty Lines.* Available at http://www.ccsd.ca/factsheets/fs_lico04_bt.htm.

Canadian Feminist Alliance for International Action. 2003. *Canada's Failure to Act: Women's Inequality Deepens.* Submission to U.N. Committee on the Elimination of Discrimination against Women on the Occasion of the Committee's Review of Canada's 5th Report. Ottawa: author.

Canadian Human Rights Commission. 2003. *Protecting Their Rights: A Systemic Review of Human Rights in Correctional Services for Federally Sentenced Women.* Ottawa: author.

Canadian Mortgage and Housing Corporation. 2003. *2003 Canadian Housing Observer. The State of Canada's Housing: An Overview.* Available at http://www.cmhc.ca/en/cahoob/stcaho/

Carlen, P. 2003. 'Virginia, Criminology, and the Antisocial Control of Women.' In *Punishment and Social Control*, ed. T. Blomberg and S. Cohen, 117–32. New York: Aldine de Gruyter.

– 1990. *Alternatives to Women's Imprisonment.* Milton Keynes: Open University Press.

– 1988. *Women, Crime and Poverty.* Milton Keynes: Open University Press.

– (ed.). 2002. *Women and Punishment: The Struggle for Justice.* Devon: William Publishing.

Chan, J., and Ericson, R. 1985. 'Decarceration and the Economy of Penal Reform.' In *New Criminologies in Canada: Crime, State and Control*, ed. T. Fleming, 223–41. Toronto: Oxford University Press.

Chan, W., and Rigakos, G. 2002. 'Risk, Crime and Gender.' *British Journal of Criminology* 42: 743–61.

Chesney-Lind, M. 2002. 'Imprisoning Women: The Unintended Victims of Mass Imprisonment.' In *Invisible Punishment: The Collateral Consequences of Mass Imprisonment*, ed. M. Mauer and M. Chesney-Lind, 79–94. New York: New Press.

Chesney-Lind, M., and Faith, K. 2001.'What about Feminism? Engendering

Theory-Making in Criminology.' In *Exploring Criminals and Crime*, ed. R. Paternoster and R. Bauchman, 287–302. Los Angeles: Roxbury Press.

Chesney-Lind, M., and Pollock, J. 1995. 'Women's Prisons: Equality with a Vengeance.' In *Women, Law, and Social Control*, ed. A. Merlo and J. Pollock, 155–75. Needham Heights: Allyn and Bacon.

Christie, N. 2000. *Crime Control as Industry: Towards Gulags, Western Style*. New York: Routledge.

– 1981. *Limits to Pain*. Oxford: Martin Robertson.

Clement, W., and Myles, J. 1994. *Relations of Ruling: Class and Gender in Postindustrial Societies*. Montreal: McGill-Queen's University Press.

Cloward, R., and Ohlin, L. 1960. *Delinquency and Opportunity*. Glencoe, IL: Free Press.

Cohen, A. 1955. *Delinquent Boys*. Glencoe, IL: Free Press.

Cohen, S. 1987. 'Taking Decentralization Seriously: Values, Visions and Policies.' In *Transcarceration: Essays in the Sociology of Social Control*, ed. J. Lowman, R. Menzies, and T. Palys, 358–79. Aldershot: Gower.

– 1985. *Visions of Social Control*. Cambridge: Polity.

Collins, P.H. 1991. *Black Feminist Thought: Knowledge, Consciousness and the Politics of Empowerment*. London: Routledge.

Comack, E. 1996. *Women in Trouble: Connecting Women's Law Violations to Their Histories of Abuse*. Halifax: Fernwood.

Comack, E., and Balfour, G. 2004. *The Power to Criminalize: Violence, Inequality and the Law*. Halifax: Fernwood.

Conrad, P., and Schneider, J. 1985. *Deviance and Medicalization: From Badness to Sickness*. Columbus, OH: Merrill Publishing Company.

Correctional Service Canada. 2005. *Basic Facts about the Correctional Service of Canada*. Ottawa: Public Works and Government Services Canada.

– 1995. *Overviews: Correctional Service of Canada Regional Facilities for Federally Sentenced Women*. Ottawa: author.

Daly, K. 1994. 'Criminal Law and Justice System Practices as Racist, White and Racialized.' *Washington and Lee Law Review* 51(2): 431–64.

Daly, K., and Chesney-Lind, M. 1988. 'Feminism and Criminology.' *Justice Quarterly* 5(4): 497–538.

Daly, K., and Maher, L. (eds.). 1998. *Criminology at the Crossroads: Feminist Readings in Crime and Justice*. New York: Oxford University Press.

Davies, S., and Cook, S. 1999. 'Neglect or Punishment? Failing to Meet the Needs of Women Post-Release.' In *Harsh Punishment: International Experiences of Women's Imprisonment*, ed. S. Cook, and S. Davies, 272–90. Boston: Northeastern University Press.

Davis, A. 2003. *Are Prisons Obsolete?* New York: Seven Stories Press.

Davis, N.J., and Faith, K. 1987. 'Women and the State: Changing Models of Social Control.' In *Transcarceration: Essays in the Sociology of Social Control*, ed. J. Lowman, et al., 170–87. Aldershot: Gower.

DeKeseredy, W. 2000. *Women, Crime, and the Canadian Criminal Justice System*. Cincinnatti: Anderson Publishing.

DeKeseredy, W., Alvi, S., Schwartz, M., and Tomaszewski, A. 2003. *Under Siege: Poverty and Crime in a Canadian Public Housing Community*. Lanham, MD: Lexington Press.

DeKeseredy, W., and Schwartz, M. 2004. 'Masculinities and Interpersonal Violence.' In *The Handbook of Studies on Men and Masculinities*, ed. M. Kimmel, R. Connell, and J. Hearn, 353–66. Thousand Oaks, CA: Sage.

– 1996. *Contemporary Criminology*. Belmont: Wadsworth.

Dell, C., and Boe, R. 1998. *Adult Female Offenders in Canada: Recent Trends*. Ottawa: Correctional Service of Canada.

DeVault, M. 1996. 'Talking Back to Sociology: Distinctive Contributions of Feminist Methodology.' *Annual Review of Sociology* 22: 29–50.

DisAbled Women's Network Ontario. *Justice with Dignity : Remember Kimberly Rogers*. Available at: http://dawn.thot.net/Kimberly_Rogers/

Eaton, M. 1993. *Women after Prison*. Buckingham: Open University Press.

Eden, D. 2002. *Inquest into the Death of Kimberly Rogers: Jury Recommendations*. Available at: http://dawn.thot.net/Kimberly_Rogers/

Ehrenreich, B. 2001. *Nickel and Dimed: On (Not) Getting By in America*. New York: Metropolitan Books.

Evening Telegram. 1995. 'Back in the World: A Special Report,' 6 May, 17.

Express. 1994. 'Women's Lock-up Called Inhumane.' 16 Nov., 1.

Faith, K. 1993. *Unruly Women: The Politics of Confinement and Resistance*. Vancouver: Press Gang.

Feeley, M., and Simon, J. 1992. 'The New Penology: Notes on the Emerging Strategy of Corrections and its Implications.' *Criminology* 30(4): 449–75.

Filmore, C., Dell, C., and Elizabeth Fry Society of Manitoba. 2001. *Prairie Women, Violence and Self-Harm*. Winnipeg.

Foucault, M. 1977. *Discipline and Punish: The Birth of the Prison*. New York: Pantheon.

Frigon, S. 2003. *L'homicide conjugal au féminin: D'hier à aujourd'hui*. Montreal: Éditions du Remue-ménage.

– 2001. 'Femmes et emprisonnement: Le marquage du corps et l'automutilation.' *Criminologie* 34(2): 31–56.

Frigon, S. and Viau, L. 2000. 'Les femmes condamnées pour homicide et l'*Examen de la légitime défense* (rapport Ratushny): Portée juridique et sociale.' *Criminologie* 33(1): 97–119.

Gendreau, P., and Ross, R. 1987. 'Revivification of rehabilitation: Evidence from the 1980s.' *Justice Quarterly* 4: 349–408.

Gendreau, P. Goggin, C., and Little, T. 1996. *Adult Recidivism: What Works!* Research Report 1996–01. Ottawa: Ministry of the Solicitor General of Canada.

George, A. 1999. 'The New Prison Culture: Making Millions from Misery.' In *Harsh Punishment: International Experiences of Women's Imprisonment*, ed. S. Cook and S. Davies, 189–210. Boston: Northeastern University Press.

Gilliom, J. 2001. *Overseers of the Poor: Surveillance, Resistance, and the Limits of Privacy.* London: University of Chicago Press.

Goffman, E. 1961. *Asylums: Essays on the Social Situation of Mental Patients and Other Inmates.* New York: Anchor Books.

Hadley, K. 2001. *And We Still Ain't Satisfied: Gender Inequality in Canada – A Status Report for 2001.* Toronto: National Action Committee on the Status of Women.

Hallinan, J. 2001. *Going Up the River: Travels in a Prison Nation.* New York: Random House.

Hamelin, M. 1989. *Femmes et prison.* Montreal: Méridien.

Hannah-Moffat, K. 2001. *Punishment in Disguise: Penal Governance and Federal Imprisonment of Women in Canada.* Toronto: University of Toronto Press.

– 2000. 'Prisons that Empower: Neo-liberal Governance in Canadian Women's Prisons.' *British Journal of Criminology* 40: 510–31.

– 1995. 'Feminine Fortresses: Women-Centered Prisons?' *Prison Journal* 75(2): 135–64.

Hannah-Moffat, K., and Shaw, M. 2003. 'The Meaning of "Risk" in Women's Prisons: A Critique.' In *Gendered Justice: Addressing Female Offenders*, ed. B. Bloom, 45–68. Durham: Carolina Academic Press.

– (eds.). 2000. 'Introduction.' In *An Ideal Prison: Critical Essays on Women's Imprisonment in Canada*, ed. K. Hannah-Moffat and M. Shaw, 11–27. Halifax: Fernwood.

Haraway, D. 1996. 'Situated Knowledges: The Science Question in Feminism and the Privilege of Partial Perspective.' *Feminism and Science*, 249–63.

– 1991. *Simians, Cyborgs and Women: The Reinvention of Nature.* New York: Routledge and Kegan Paul.

Hartsock, N. 1998. *The Feminist Standpoint Revisited, and Other Essays.* Boulder, CO: Westview.

Hattem, T. 1991. 'Vivre avec ses peines.' *Déviance et Société* 15(2): 137–56.

Heidensohn, F. 1987. 'Women and Crime: Questions for Criminology.' In *Gender, Crime and Justice*, ed. P. Carlen and A. Worrall, 16–27. Philadelphia: Open University Press.

Heisz, A., and McLeod, L. 2004. 'Low Income in Census Metropolitan Areas.' *Perspectives on Labour and Income* 5(5). Ottawa: Statistics Canada.

Heney, J. 1990. *Report on Self-injurious Behaviour in the Kingston Prison for Women*. Ottawa: Ministry of the Solicitor General.

Heney, J., and Kristiansen, C. 1998. 'An Analysis of the Impact of Prison on Women Survivors of Childhood Sexual Abuse.' In *Breaking the Rules: Women in Prison and Feminist Therapy*, ed. J. Harden and A. Hill, 29–45. New York: Haworth Press.

Hermer, J., and Mosher, J. (eds.). 2002. *Disorderly People: Law and the Politics of Exclusion in Ontario*. Halifax: Fernwood.

Hertz, R. 1997. *Reflexivity and Voice*. Thousand Oaks, CA: Sage.

Horii, G. 2000. 'Processing Humans.' In *An Ideal Prison: Critical Essays on Women's Imprisonment in Canada*, ed. K. Hannah-Moffat and M. Shaw, 104–16. Halifax: Fernwood.

Hughes, S. 1991. *Report of the Royal Commission of Inquiry into the Criminal Justice System*. St John's: Queen's Printer, Government of Newfoundland.

Human Development Index. 2004. *United Nations Development Programme*. Available at: http://hdr.undp.org/statistics/data/

Human Resources and Development Canada. 2005. *Current and Forthcoming Minimum Hourly Wage Rate for Experienced Adult Workers in Canada*. Ottawa: Government of Canada.

Income Security Advocacy Centre. 2003. *Ontario Lifetime Ban Statistics*. Available at http://www.incomesecurity.org

Ingleby, D. 1983. 'Mental Health and Social Order.' In *Social Control and the State*, ed. S. Cohen and A. Scull, 141–88. New York: St Martin's Press.

Jaccoud, M. 1992. 'Les femmes autochtones et la justice pénale.' *Criminologie* 25(1): 65–85.

Jaggar, A. 1983. *Feminist Politics and Human Nature*. Totowa, NJ: Rowman and Allanheld.

Jhappan, R. (ed.). 2002. *Women's Legal Strategies in Canada*. Toronto: University of Toronto Press.

Johnson, R., and Toch, H. (eds.). 1982. *The Pains of Imprisonment*. Beverly Hills, CA: Sage.

Jousten, M., and Zvekic, U. 1994. 'Noncustodial Sanctions: Comparative Overview.' In *Alternatives to Imprisonment in Comparative Perspective.*, ed. U. Zvekic, 1–42. Chicago: Nelson Hall.

Kaiser, A. 2004. *The Criminalization of People with Mental Health Problems: Joining Together to Find a Way Forward*. Ottawa: NAACJ / Justice Canada / Public Safety and Emergency Preparedness Joint Policy Forum: Human Rights of People with Mental Disabilities and the Criminal Justice System.

Keller, E. 1996. In *Feminism and Science*, ed. E. Keller and H. Longino. New York: Oxford University Press.

Kemshall, H. 2002. 'Effective Practice in Probation: An Example of "Advanced Liberal" Responsibilisation.' *Howard Journal* 41(1): 41–58.

Kendall, K. 2004. 'Dangerous Thinking: A Critical History of Correctional Cognitive Behaviouralism.' In *What Matters in Probation*, ed. G. Mair, 53–89. Devon: William Publishing.

– 2000. 'Psy-ence Fiction: Governing Female Prisons through the Psychological Services.' In *An Ideal Prison: Critical Essays on Women's Imprisonment in Canada*, ed. K. Hannah-Moffat and M. Shaw, 82–93. Halifax: Fernwood.

Kirby, S., and McKenna, K. 1989. *Methods from the Margins: Experience, Research, Social Change*. Toronto: Garamond.

Lofland, J., and Lofland, L. 1984. *Analyzing Social Settings*. Belmont, CA: Wadsworth.

Lowman, J., Menzies, R.J., and Palys, T.S. 1987. 'Introduction: Transcarceration and the Modern State of Penality.' In *Transcarceration: Essays in the Sociology of Social Control*, ed. J. Lowman et al., 1–18. Aldershot: Gower.

Lurigio, A. 2001. 'Effective Services for Parolees with Mental Illnesses.' *Crime and Delinquency* 47(3): 446–61.

Luther, D. 2003. *Report of Inquiries into the Sudden Deaths of Norman Edward Reid and Darryl Brandon Power*. St John's: Government of Newfoundland and Labrador.

MacKinnon, C. 1982. 'Feminism, Marxism, Method, and the State: An Agenda for Theory.' *Signs* 7: 515–44.

MacLeod, L. 1986. *Sentenced to Separation: An Exploration of the Needs and Problems of Mothers Who Are Offenders and Their Children*. Ottawa: Solicitor General Canada.

Maidment, M. 2002. 'Toward a Woman-Centered Approach to Community-Based Corrections: A Gendered Analysis of Women and Electronic Monitoring.' *Women and Criminal Justice* 13(4): 47–68.

Mainprize, S. 1992. 'Electronic Monitoring in Corrections: Assessing Cost Effectiveness and the Potential for Widening the Net of Social Control.' *Canadian Journal of Criminology* 34(2): 161–80.

Majury, D. 2002. 'Women's (In)Equality before and after the Charter.' In *Women's Legal Strategies in Canada*, ed. R. Jhappan. 101–34. Toronto: University of Toronto Press.

Manitoba, Aboriginal Justice Inquiry. 1991. *Justice on Trial: Report of the Aboriginal Justice Inquiry*. Winnipeg: Queen's Press.

Mann, C. 1993. *Unequal Justice: A Question of Color*. Bloomington: Indiana University Press.

Martel, J. 1999. *Solitude and Cold Storage: Women's Journeys of Endurance in Segregation*. Edmonton: Elizabeth Fry Society of Edmonton.

Martin, D. 2002. 'Demonizing Youth, Marketing Fear: The New Politics of Crime.' In *Disorderly People: Law and the Politics of Exclusion in Ontario*, ed. J. Hermer and J. Mosher, 91–104. Halifax: Fernwood Publishing.

Matthews, R. 1987. 'Decarceration and Social Control: Fantasies and Realities.' In *Transcarceration: Essays in the Sociology of Social Control*, ed. J. Lowman et al., 101–98. Aldershot: Gower.

Mauthner, N., and Doucet, A. 1998. 'Reflections on a Voice-Centered Relational Method: Analysing Maternal and Domestic Voices.' In *Feminist Dilemmas in Qualitative Research: Public Knowledge and Private Lives*, ed. J. Ribbens and R. Edwards, 119–44. London: Sage.

McCold, P., and Wachtel, B. 1998. 'Community Is Not a Place: A New Look at Community Justice Initiatives.' *Contemporary Justice Review* 1: 71–85.

McCormick, K., and L. Visano, 1992. 'Corrections and Community (In)Action.' In *Canadian Penology*, ed. K. McCormick and L. Visano, 275–90. Toronto: Canadian Scholars' Press.

McGee, S. 2000. 'The Pains of Imprisonment: Long-Term Incarceration Effects on Women in Prison.' In *It's a Crime: Women and Justice*, ed. R. Muraskin, 205–13. Englewood Cliffs, NJ: Prentice-Hall.

Merton, R. 1938. 'Social Structure and Anomie.' *American Sociological Review* 3: 672–82.

Messerschmidt, J. 1986. *Capitalism, Patriarchy, and Crime: Toward a Socialist Feminist Criminology*. Totowa, NJ: Rowman and Littlefield.

Micucci, A., Maidment, M., and Gomme, I. 1997. 'Cleaner than I Ever Was: The Experiences of Female Offenders in a Monitored Conditional Release Program in Eastern Canada.' *Journal of Offender Monitoring* 10(1): 1–11.

Miller, S. (ed.). 1998. *Crime Control and Women: Feminist Implications of Criminal Justice Policy*. Thousand Oaks, CA.: Sage.

Mills, C.W. 1959. *The Sociological Imagination*. New York: Oxford University Press.

Monster, M. 2000. '"There's Nothing Offered Here": The Rhetoric and Reality of a Rehabilitative Approach at the Newfoundland and Labrador Correctional Centre for Women.' Unpublished Master's thesis, Department of Sociology, Memorial University of Newfoundland.

Morash, M., and Schram, P. 2002. *The Prison Experience: Special Issues of Women in Prison*. Prospect Hills, IL: Waveland Press.

Mosher, J. 2002. 'The Shrinking of the Public and Private Spaces of the Poor.' In *Disorderly People: Law and the Politics of Exclusion in Ontario*, ed. J. Hermer and J. Mosher, 41–53. Halifax: Fernwood.

Mosher, J., Evans, P., Little, M., Ontario Association of Interval Houses, and Ontario Social Safety Network. 2004. *Walking on Eggshells: Abused Women's Experiences of Ontario's Welfare System.* Final Report of Research Findings from the Woman and Abuse Research Project.

Motiuk, L., and Blanchette, K. 1998. Assessing Female Offenders: What Works? Paper presented to the International Community Corrections Association, Annual Conference, Arlington, Virginia.

Naffine, N. 1996. *Feminism and Criminology.* Philadelphia: Temple University Press.

Neve, L., and Pate, K. 2005. 'Challenging the Criminalization of Women Who Resist.' In *Global Lockdown: Race, Gender and the Prison Industrial Complex,* ed. J. Sudbury, 19–33. New York: Routledge.

Newfoundland and Labrador, Department of Health. 2004. *OxyContin Task Force: Final Report.* St John's: Queen's Printer.

Newfoundland and Labrador, Department of Justice. 2001. *Bi-Annual Report: Division of Corrections and Community Services.* St John's: Queen's Printer.

Newfoundland and Labrador, Statistics Agency. 2004. *Government of Newfoundland and Labrador.* Accessed at http://www.stats.gov.nl.ca/

Nielsen, M., and Silverman, R. 1996. *Native Americans, Crime, and Justice.* Boulder, CO: Westview.

O'Brien, D. 1991. *Suffer Little Children: An Autobiography of a Foster Child.* St John's: Breakwater Books.

O'Brien, P. 2001. *Making It in the 'Free World': Women in Transition from Prison.* Albany: State University of New York Press.

O'Grady, B., and Blight, R. 2002. 'Squeezed to the Point of Exclusion: The Case of Toronto Squeegee Cleaners.' In *Disorderly People: Law and the Politics of Exclusion in Ontario,* ed. J. Hermer and J. Mosher, 23–39. Halifax: Fernwood.

O'Malley, P. 2000. 'Risk Societies and the Government of Crime.' In *Dangerousness, Risk and Modern Society,* ed. M. Brown and J. Pratt. London: Routledge.

Parent, C. 1998. *Féminismes et criminologie.* Paris and Brussells: De Boeck University.

Pate, K. 2003. 'A Tribute to Gayle Horii.' *Journal of Prisoners on Prisons* 12: 163–9.

Peters, Y. 2003. *Federally Sentenced Women with Mental Disabilities: A Dark Corner in Canadian Human Rights.* Ottawa: DisAbled Women's Action Network Canada.

Petersilia, J. 2003. *When Prisoners Come Home: Parole and Prisoner Reentry.* New York: Oxford University Press.

Pimlott, S., and Sarri, R. 2002. 'The Forgotten Group: Women in Prisons and Jails.' In *Women at the Margins: Neglect, Punishment, and Resistance,* ed. J. Figueira-McDonough and R. Sarri, 55–85. London: Haworth Press.

Pollack, S. 2000. 'Reconceptualizing Women's Agency and Empowerment: Challenges to Self-Esteem Discourse and Women's Lawbreaking.' *Women and Criminal Justice* 12(1): 75–89.

Pollack, S., and Kendall, K. 2005. 'Taming the Shrew: Regulating Prisoners through Women-Centered Mental Health Programming.' *Critical Criminology* 13: 71–87.

Quinney, R. 1970. *The Social Reality of Crime*. Boston: Little, Brown.

Raphael, J. 2000. *Saving Bernice: Battered Women, Welfare, and Poverty*. Boston: Northeastern University Press.

Reiman, J. 2004. *The Rich Get Richer and the Poor Get Prison: Ideology, Class and Criminal Justice*. Needham Heights, MA.: Allyn and Bacon.

Renzetti, C., Edleson, J., and Bergen, R. (eds.). 2001. *Sourcebook on Violence against Women*. Thousand Oaks, CA: Sage.

Richie, B. 2001. 'Challenges Incarcerated Women Face as They Return to Their Communities: Findings from Life History Interviews.' *Crime and Delinquency* 47(3): 368–89.

Ristock, J., and Pennell, J. 1996. *Community Research as Empowerment: Feminist Links, Postmodern Interruptions*. New York: Oxford University Press.

Ross, R., and Gendreau, P. 1980. *Effective Correctional Treatment*. Toronto: Butterworths.

Rossiter, H. 2001. 'Female Offenders in the Newfoundland Penitentiary System, 1990–2000: A Cross-Sectional Profile and Emergent Trends.' Unpublished honours' dissertation, Department of Sociology, Memorial University of Newfoundland.

Rothman, D. 1980. *Conscience and Convenience: The Asylum and Its Alternatives in Progressive America*. Boston: Little, Brown.

Schur, E. 1984. *Labeling Women Deviant: Gender, Stigma, and Social Control*. New York: Random House.

Schwandt, T. 2001. *Dictionary of Qualitative Inquiry*. Thousand Oaks, CA: Sage.

Scraton, P. 1990. 'Scientific Knowledge or Masculine Discourses? Challenging Patriarchy in Criminology.' In *Feminist Perspectives in Criminology*, ed. L. Gelsthorpe and A. Morris, 10–25. Milton Keynes: Open University Press.

Scull, A. 1977. *Decarceration: Community Treatment and the Deviant – A Radical View*. Englewood Cliffs, NJ: Prentice-Hall.

Seymour, P., and Greene, J. 2000. *A Community Strategy for Federally Sentenced Women on Conditional Release: Phase II Project Report*. St John's: n.p.

Shaw, M. 1994. 'Women in Prison: A Literature Review.' *Forum on Corrections Research* 6(1): 13–18.

Shaw, M., and Hannah-Moffat, K. 2004. 'How Cognitive Skills Forgot about

Gender and Diversity.' In *What Matters in Probation*, ed. G. Mair, 90–121. Devon: William Publishing.

Simon, R. 1975. *Women and Crime*. Lexington, MA: Lexington Books.

Smart, C. 1998. *Feminism and the Power of Law*. London: Routledge.

– 1990.'Feminist Approaches to Criminology or Postmodern Woman Meets Atavistic Man.' In *Feminist Perspectives in Criminology*, ed. L. Gelsthorpe and A. Morris, 70–84. Milton Keynes: Open University Press.

Smith, D. 1987. *The Everyday World as Problematic: A Feminist Sociology*. Milton Keynes: Open University Press.

Solomon, H. 1976. *Community Corrections*. Boston: Holbrook Press.

Stanley, L., and Wise, S. 1983. *Breaking Out: Feminist Consciousness and Feminist Research*. London: Routledge and Kegan Paul.

Statistics Canada. 2004. *Labour Force Survey*. Ottawa: author.

St John's Status of Women Council. 2003. *Something's Got to Change – Research Report: Gender Inclusive Analysis and Housing Policy Development in Newfoundland and Labrador*. St John's: author.

Strategic Social Plan. 2004. *Community Accounts Profile*. St John's: Government of Newfoundland and Labrador. Available at www.communityaccounts.ca.

Sudbury, J. (ed.). 2005. *Global Lockdown: Race, Gender and the Prison Industrial Complex*. New York: Routledge.

Sweet, B. 2003. 'Cry for Help: Judge Denies Abuse Victims' Request for Federal Time.' *St John's Telegram*, 24 June, A1.

Sykes, G. 1958. *The Society of Captives: A Study of Maximum Security Prison*. Princeton, NJ: Princeton University Press.

Task Force on Federally Sentenced Women. 1990. *Creating Choices: Report of the Task Force on Federally Sentenced Women*. Ottawa: Ministry of the Solicitor General.

Tong, R. 1998. *Feminist Thought: A More Comprehensive Introduction*. Boulder, CO: Westview.

United Nations. 1998. *Human Development Report, 1998*. Toronto: Oxford University Press.

Van Wormer, K. 2003. 'Prison Privatization and Women.' In *Capitalist Punishment: Prison Privatization and Human Rights*, ed. A. Coyle, A. Campbell, and R. Neufeld, 102–13. Atlanta: Clarity Press.

Waquant, L. 2003. 'America's New "Peculiar Institution": On the Prison as Surrogate Ghetto.' In *Punishment and Social Control*, ed. T. Blomberg and S. Cohen, 471–82. New York: Aline de Gruyter.

– 2001. 'The Penalisation of Poverty and the Rise of Neo-Liberalism.' *European Journal on Criminal Policy and Research* 9: 401–12.

Warren, C. 1981. 'New Forms of Social Control: The Myth of Deinstitutionalization.' *American Behavioural Scientist* 24(6): 724–40.

Watson, L. 1995. 'In the Best Interest of the Child: The Mother-Child Program.' *Forum on Corrections Research* 7(2): 25–7.

Websdale, N. 1998. *Rural Woman Battering and the Justice System: An Ethnography.* Thousand Oaks, CA: Sage.

Welch, M. 1997. 'Regulating the Reproduction and Morality of Women: The Social Control of Body and Soul.' *Women and Criminal Justice* 9(1): 17–38.

Western Star. 1997. 'Money Made Available to Establish Elizabeth Fry Society in Province,' 10 May.

Wilson, W.J. 1996. *When Work Disappears: The World of the New Urban Poor.* New York: Knopf.

Wolf, D. (ed.) 1996. *Feminist Dilemmas in Fieldwork.* Boulder, CO: Westview.

Women's Issues Task Force. 1995. *Women's Voices: Women's Choices – Report of the Women's Issues Task Force.* Toronto: Ontario Ministry of Correctional Services.

Worrall, A. 1997. *Punishment in the Community: The Future of Criminal Justice.* London: Longman.

Young, J. 1999. *The Exclusive Society.* London: Sage.

Index

Aboriginal, 37, 110; healing practices, 29; women, 16, 27, 41, 43, 62, 67–8, 105

Aboriginal Justice Inquiry (Manitoba), 41

abuse, 13, 50, 55, 93, 97, 133, 149, 151; in fostering arrangements, 74; high rates of, 68; from a male partner, 59, 103–4, 109, 111, 117; past, 69, 72–4, 76, 92, 119; physical, 11–12, 67, 117–18, 122, 146, 150; sexual, 12, 37, 44, 59, 67–71, 86, 109, 115, 122, 146, 150; substance, 48, 72, 82, 88, 100, 117; of young boys, 70, 111–12

addiction, 43, 68, 76, 109, 151; and prescription medications, 72, 92, 135. *See also* abuse, substance; alcohol; drugs

Alberta, 41

alcohol (problems), 37, 53–4, 72–3, 80, 95, 117

androcentrism, 19, 23–4, 26, 37, 51. *See also* men

Antigonish, 85

antisocial: behaviour, 49; control, 49, 72, 74, 78, 80, 129; definition of, 124–5; family, 125

Arbour Commission, 3, 43–4

Atlantic Canada: incidence of low weekly wages, 59; prisons in, 30, 42

British Columbia, 41, 75

Bull Arm, 107

Canadian Feminist Alliance for International Action, 46

Canadian Mental Health Association, 88, 112

Carew Lodge, 141

case management, 5, 112; assertive,15, 18, 135–6, 141–2, 145

Charter of Rights and Freedoms (Canada), 45, 149–50

cheque forging, 39

child, 81, 114–15; care responsibilities, 44, 50, 60, 108, 119, 151; custody and care mangle, 74, 77; molester, 71; protection agencies, 5, 18, 31, 69–70, 74–7, 123, 129, 135–9, 143, 146; removed from mother, 69, 72, 76, 78; unborn, 45. *See also* poverty

Child Welfare, 69, 76–7, 135

Child and Youth Family Services, 137

children, 4, 21, 42, 46, 60–1, 78, 80, 83, 99, 104, 108, 113–15, 119, 149, 151; abused in foster care, 69; placed for adoption, 137; custody of, 5, 66, 137; and geographical isolation from mother, 83, 89; reconciliation with the mother, 136; reuniting with, 4, 103; teenage, 113; as victims, 41; young, 66, 68–9. *See also* foster care

Clarenville, 47, 83–7, 90, 94, 96

class, 9–10, 16, 19–22, 24, 26, 34, 37, 60, 79, 81

Cohen, S., 17–19, 124–5, 127–8

College of the North Atlantic, 84

community, 3–14, 31, 50, 88–9, 96, 110, 146; Aboriginal, 63; -based reforms, 3, 125–6, 148, 151–2; control, 17–18; corrections, 29–30; groups, 6; meaning of the term, 10, 17–18, 126, 139; mental health services, 88, 124, 128; programs, lack of, 111; punishment in the, 14, 152; regulatory, 18; release into the, 146; as repressive site, 32; rural, 104; service order, 30; treatment, 17, 112, 127; treatment order, 112. *See also* local level; social control

conditional: release, 4–5, 7, 28–9, 48, 51, 112; sentence, 5, 85. *See also* house arrest; probation; parole; surveillance

confinement: involuntary, 89; solitary, 17, 44, 127–8. *See also* psychiatric hospital

control talk, 15, 31

Correctional Service of Canada, 28, 38, 47, 52, 143

corrections (system), 5, 15–16, 27–30, 129; business of, 133; inequalities in, 18; knowledge-legitimation processes of, 52; repressive tool of the state, 3; research, 6, 11, 47–56; staff, 49, 120; theory, 48; woman-centred, 3–4, 26, 29, 38, 83, 143. *See also* gender; imprisonment; prison

Corrections Canada, 28, 144

counselling, 6, 70, 90, 105, 111, 133, 138, 144, 147; on abuse, 82, 133; barriers to, 140; employment, 95–6; mandatory, 109; professional, 119–21; program, 48

Creating Choices: Task Force on Federally Sentenced Women, 28–9, 38, 42, 46

Criminal Code, 83

criminal justice system, 3–6, 8, 11–12, 14–18, 25, 28, 30–1, 34, 36–9, 46, 50–2, 58, 68, 70, 74–5, 81, 88–9, 106, 114, 123–5, 127–9, 131–3, 139, 141, 143, 148, 151–2; gender-blind, 10; reputation of, 16

criminality, cycle of, 7; women's, 33–4, 109

criminalization, 21, 33–7, 63, 77; effects of, 44; of ethnicity, 16; links with abuse, 68; of mental illness, 12, 19, 26, 88–95, 150; patterns of, 73; of race, 16, 27–8; of poverty, 16, 36, 59–60, 148; trajectory of, 57; of women, 7, 12, 16–17, 19, 38, 43, 45, 82, 115, 152; of youth, 36

criminalized: men, 5, 30, 83; populations, 7, 28–9, 31; women, 3–5, 7–8, 10–12, 14–17, 37, 41, 43–4, 46, 48–9, 51, 53–4, 59, 65, 67, 72, 74, 76, 83, 95, 105–6, 109–11, 118, 148, 150

criminalizing women, 33–46, 50; factors contributing to, 4
criminology, 26; androcentric, 151; critical, 33–4; feminist, 19–24, 150; transgressive, 148, 150
custody: 7, 12, 19, 26, 69, 74, 88, 90, ˙126; gender-based approach to, 43; open, 76. *See also* imprisonment; release from prison; return to prison; staying out of prison

decarceration, 19, 32, 125–6, 129; of mental patients, 128; movement, 31; strategies of, 127
deinstitutionalization, 19, 89, 127, 129
dependency (culture of), 6, 37, 81, 96, 121, 133, 142, 147, 151
depression, 55, 63, 72, 93; post-natal, 77
discourse, correctional, 7, 11, 14, 25, 33, 36, 54, 150. *See also* language
drugs, 26, 63, 72–3, 92, 94–5, 100, 117–18, 134; prescription, 93, 133, 135; psychoactive, 19, 126. *See also* medication

education, 4, 11, 21–2, 34, 53, 56, 58–9, 64, 67, 75, 80, 87, 106, 111, 124, 151; and crime, relationship, 72–3
Elizabeth Fry Society/ies: Canadian Association of, 10, 26, 42–3, 46, 51, 63, 73; of Manitoba, 44, 57, 67, 69; of Newfoundland and Labrador, 10, 48, 141
empiricism, feminist, 24
employment, 4, 11–12, 41, 65, 87, 147; counselling, 82, 95–6; horizontal and vertical segregation of, 107; market, 33, 62; meaningful, 4, 106–11; skills, 106, 108, 113

empowerment, 3, 29, 64, 101, 123–4, 145; economic, 151; rationale of, 144; social, 81, 151
England, 36, 44
epistemologies, feminist, 8, 19, 25–6
equality, 16, 42–3, 83, 150; defined, 38; formal, 12, 33, 37–8, 83; sexual, 37; substantive, 12, 33, 37–8, 152. *See also* inequality
ethnicity, 9, 16, 41, 53
Eurocentrism, 22
Exchange of Services Agreement, 47, 83
exclusion, 6–7, 15–16, 18, 20, 34, 50, 54, 125, 151–2; axes of, 15–16, 81; of criminalized women, 49; economic, 34; politics of, 36; sexuality-based, 80–1; social, 34, 80

family, 4, 17, 20, 28–9, 33–6, 40, 42, 44, 61, 64–5, 67, 71, 76, 78, 83–5, 115–16, 121; antisocial, 125; background, 67, 74; contact complicated by distance, 42; doctor, 140–1; foster, 116, 118; ideology, 125; lone-parent, 39–40; poverty, 60; relations, 115–16, 124; responsibility, 34; size, 40; social conceptions of, 147. *See also* interpersonal relations
Family Services, 137
family supports, 55, 84, 115–18, 121, 143; lack of, 4
federal prison, 26, 30, 41, 43, 77, 121; more opportunities in, 86, 88, 94; vs provincial equality, 12; request for transfer to, 48, 84–5; sentences, 5, 47–8, 83–6, 137; women in, 3, 28–9, 38, 42, 46, 83–100;
feminism. *See* socialist feminism;

standpoint feminism; Marxist feminism

feminists, 18, 23, 25, 37, 46, 144, 150–1

foster care, 44, 55, 70, 75–7, 95, 115–16, 118, 136–7, 146; abuses while in, 69; to custody, 74

funding, 65, 110; for local groups, 17–18, 29, 32, 112, 123, 127, 143; the prison endeavour, 21, 151; for women's programs, 107

gender, 9–10, 20–4, 38, 43, 125, 147, 151–2; -blind standardized risk assessments, 8; and crime, 23, 26; deconstructing, 23; foremost in analysis of women's involvement with formal control agents, 124; gap in treatment, 109–11; -neutral standards, 37; relations, 19, 25; roles, 130; as a social construct, 21, 26, 78, 150; wage gap, 106. See also inequalities; norms

gender-based: analysis of housing policy, 61; approach to custody, 43; disparities, 38; programming, 8, 94; supports, 8, 94, 109

gendered: availability of services, 87; division of labour, 107, 152; power structure, 16; prison conditions, 87; realities, 54

gender norms, 12, 57, 59, 78–80, 107, 146, 150–1; defiance of, 78–81; violation of, 11–12

halfway house, 19, 97, 117–18, 127, 129, 143

Halifax, 85, 104, 116–17

harm reduction measures, 43

health care, 34, 88–9, 91, 150

homelessness, 12–13, 105, 149; hidden, 59, 63

house arrest, 3, 10, 45–6. See also surveillance

housing, 4, 19, 36, 43, 96–7, 146; adequate, 43, 45; affordable, 4, 12, 61, 63, 67, 103–5, 147; the 'mad' and the 'bad,' 127; needs (core), 61, 63, 103–6; public, 72, 79; rural, 104; safe, 4, 103–5, 147; and treatment programs, 144; in large urban centres, 36

human rights, 83, 149–50; abuses, 48; international, 46; laws, 43; violations of prisoners', 3, 29, 43, 151

Human Rights Act, 42

Human Rights Commission (Canada), 3, 5, 41–3, 48, 83

ideology, 7, 19, 27, 34, 38, 107; penal, 6, 29, 33, 50, 144; of preventive psychiatry and community mental health, 128. See also neoconservative; neoliberal

imprisonment, 15, 53, 76, 136; alternatives to (see also community), 28–31; costs of, 28, 31; increased, 21, 27; material and legal realities of, 3, 43–4, 81–101, 144; mother's, 44; as the norm, 30; previous, 47; psychological, 71; rates, 38, 47; and sexual abuse, 69; of single mothers, 41, 44. See also post-imprisonment; pre-imprisonment; prison; release; staying out

incarceration. See imprisonment

inequality, 15, 20, 22, 50, 148, 152; class, 34; in corrections, 18; cultural, 82; economic, 82; ethnic, 22; gender, 22, 34, 80; income, 36; political, 82; racial, 22, 34; social, 152; systemic, 4, 8, 12, 16, 18, 28, 148

infantilization, 6, 101, 147

institutionalization: of mental patients, 128, 141; of women, 7, 12, 52, 95–102, 119, 121; when long-standing and prevalent, 116

International Covenant: on Civil and Political Rights, 46; on Economic and Social Rights, 46

interpersonal relationships, 6, 12; familial, 115–17; intimate, 117–19; professional, 119–22; renegotiating, 115–19. *See also* family; support system

intervention (by state), 18, 69–70, 127, 130, 136–7

Inuit, 105. *See also* Aboriginal

Irish Christian Brothers, 69

Janeway Children's Hospital, 70, 135

job, 45, 58–9, 62–3, 65, 104, 106–8, 128. *See also* employment

justice. *See* criminal justice system; social justice

knowledge, 31, 102, 150; androcentric, 19, 26; construction of, 11, 49–50, 53; deconstruction of, 19, 23–4; legitimation, 24–5; official vs marginal, 52; and power, 22, 25; recreation, 56. *See also* empiricism; epistemologies

labelling (process), 9, 17, 78–9, 114, 146

language, 6–7, 143–4; and control, 14–15; correctional straitjacket imposed by, 7; deconstruction of, 14–17; as management tool, 17–18; penal, 6, 16; of 'treatment,' 31

local level, 82; alternatives to prison, 29–32; controls, 4–6, 12, 30, 58, 123–45; corrections, 4, 19, 27; initiatives, 30–1, 46; mental health services, 88; neighbourhood, 145; programs, 32, 43; reform, 3; release to, 54, 82; services, 42–3, 131; strategies, 29; supports, 111, 139–40

local organizations, 5–6, 17–19, 110, 133, 135, 143; absorbed by formal state apparatus, 17, 19, 29, 32. *See also* community; non-profit organizations

Low Income Cut-offs, 39–40, 64

Luther Inquiry, 111–12

Manitoba, 41, 57, 67, 69

marginality, 34, 150; penal institutions used to govern, 34

marginalization: of women (economically), 7, 20, 148

Marxist feminism, 20. *See also* socialist feminism

medicalization, 6, 101, 147, 151; of criminalized women, 8

medication, 45, 71, 84, 90, 92–3, 133, 135, 138, 140; of problems, 122. *See also* drugs

men, as the norm (comparator), 24, 83, 150–1

mental health, 35, 44, 63, 123–5, 142–3; agencies, 5–6, 12, 18, 32, 74–5, 128–33, 139, 146; arena of intervention, 70, 130; care system, 15, 88, 129, 131; detainees, 8; diagnoses, 111–12, 133, 140; legislation, 89, 111–12; 147; misdiagnosis, 135; needs, 48, 133, 139; problems, 86,

88, 90, 100; services, 86, 88, 128–31,
139, 146. *See also* abuse; addiction;
community; criminalization;
depression; psychiatry
Mental Health Act (Newfoundland),
111–12, 131–2
mental illness, 11–13, 16, 19, 43, 48,
76–7, 88–91, 93–4, 112, 134–5, 139;
deinstitutionalization of, 126; diagnosis, 88–9, 92–4
methodology, 47–56; feminist, 12, 53–
4; researching from the margins,
47, 50, 52–3, 56
military industrial complex, 125, 151
mother, 36, 71, 76–7, 80–1, 97, 110,
114–16, 136; criminalized, 138;
good, make good families, 125;
relationship with, 116; role, 10;
unfit, 130, 137. *See also* single
mother
Mount Cashel Orphanage, 69–70

Native. *See* Aboriginal
Native Friendship Centre, 105
neoconservate/ism, 12, 33–7, 129
neoliberal/ism, 6–7, 11–14, 17, 21,
26–7, 32–7, 49, 60, 65, 107, 146, 151
New Brunswick, 41
Newfoundland and Labrador, 41, 90;
conditions in, 134–5; Correctional
Centre for Women (NLCCW), 47,
84, 86–7, 94; Department of Justice,
47; housing policy, 61; justice system, 52, 83–4, 111; lack of prison
programs, 48, 83–101, 111; lone-
parent families, number of, 60;
mental health services, 65; numbers of incarcerated women, 47;
rural, 104; social assistance rates,
39–40, 46; unemployment rates, 41

non-profit agencies: replicate control,
147. *See also* local organizations
norms: beauty, 78–9; body image,
125; legal, 11–12; maternity, 80–1;
sexuality, 79; state-imposed, 96. *See
also* gender norms
Nova (women's prison in Truro), 86,
90, 96–7; desire to go back to, 87
Nova Scotia, 41–3

Ontario, 30, 35–6, 41, 45, 60, 65, 103,
149; Kingston, 42, 44–5, 60; Sudbury, 45; 'Ottawa School,' 49

parole, 4, 31, 85, 129, 134, 141; agencies, 134; breach of, 132; card, 103,
108; denied, 111; and employment, 107; hearing, 111; officer, 6,
51, 85, 111, 120; release job program, 107, 111; revocation of, 51;
services, 139; terms of, 148; untenable conditions of, 5. *See also* conditional release
parole officer, 6, 51, 85, 111; relationship with, 119–20
pathologizing women, 14–19, 51;
both inside and outside of prison,
3
patriarchy, capitalist, 11, 15–16, 24–5,
34, 36, 106, 130, 148; definition, 20;
as driving force of women's
oppression, 150–1; gender relations, 20
penal (prison): datakeeping, 52; controls, formal, 14–32, 124; goals, of
punishment and surveillance, 143.
See also ideology; language; social
control
penal industrial complex, 21, 26–32,
133; local, 143

penal institution. *See* prison; *specific prisons by name*

penal planning and management, 38, 146; rationale for, 29, 32; reform of, 3

Penal Services Among Canada, 28

penal system, 16, 41, 49–50, 59, 76, 83, 88–9, 101, 123, 129, 131, 133, 143, 147, 151. *See also* corrections

penology, 6, 10, 26; at the local level, 4. *See also* criminology

personal care homes, 18

Pleasantville, 75

police: as first agents of social control, 69–70, 84, 88, 111, 130–2, 136, 138; interference by, 111–14. *See also* surveillance

policy, 4, 28, 88–9, 104, 124; of closing down asylums, prisons, and reformatories, 126; criminal justice, 35; economic, 148; recommendations, 12–13; social, 10, 35, 152; social assistance (Ontario), 149

positionality, 54–5, 56, 65, 69, 106, 113, 152

post-imprisonment, 4–5, 12, 63, 83, 102–22, 131, 134, 138, 143. *See also* release (from prison)

poverty, 16, 28, 46, 48, 59–67, 103–4, 108, 118, 149–50; and abuse, 111; child, 39, 60; correlates, 59, 64; cycle of, 62, 72, 111; extreme, 107; feminization of, 16, 36–7, 39, 62, 148; line, 39, 59, 60, 107; and housing, 103–7; as pathway to criminality, 135, 146; patterns of, 81, 151; rates, 59; upon release, 118; and substandard living conditions, 63; stresses of, 39; trap, 57, 59–67; urban, 60; and violence, 104

pre-imprisonment, 5, 12, 74, 147. *See also* prison, pathways to

Prince Edward Island, 41

prison(s): 5–7, 10, 15, 17–18, 31–2, 38, 48, 102, 118, 127, 130; abolitionists, 143; corporatization of, 27; experiences, 69, 82–101, 135, 145; fathers in, 44; as 'home,' 52; medium security, 47; and mental health services, 131–2, 136; pathways to, 8, 12, 53–4, 57–82, 87, 115, 117, 143, 148; privatization of, 27, 129; and problems of distance from home, 41–2; rationale for funding, 29; regionalization of, 30, 42; reprisal measures taken in, 44; riot (Kingston), 44; two-tiered, 3, 12, 83, 85–8; women's, 3, 28, 150. *See also* imprisonment; post-imprisonment; pre-imprisonment; programs; release from prison; return to prison; staying out of prison; *names of specific prisons*

prison conditions, 93; gendered, 87; inhumanity of, 99, 101

prisoning, 7, 12, 57; of women, 82–101

probation, 4, 6, 30–1, 45, 48, 51, 82, 129, 133, 141; and labelling process, 114

probation officer, 6, 121, 134; relationship with, 119–20

programs, prison, 38, 48, 51, 82–101, 107–11; design and delivery, 144; federal, counselling, 48; not gender-specific, 109; offloaded onto local agencies, 110; shortage of in women's prisons, 87; geared to specific offences, 95; for substance abuse, 85, 88; unavailable through

provincial sentence, 85, 95; upon
release, 85, 95, 107–8; for women
who have no family, 115
protective custody, 90
Provincial Court, Mental Health
Division, 112
provincial government, 47–8, 52; fiscal policies, 65
provincial prison, 12, 38, 48, 83, 85,
87, 94, 99; expenditures, 28; lack of
programs in, 83–7, 94; sentences,
47–8, 83, 85; for women, 47
psychiatric hospital, 52, 69, 75, 92, 97,
114, 120, 130, 133–4; confinement
in, 97, 147
psychiatric illness, 19, 53–4, 76, 98,
114, 133, 140, 142. See also mental
illness
psychiatrist, 75, 77, 89–90, 92, 95, 99,
120–1, 132, 140–1
psychiatry, 4, 6, 17, 146; as social control, 123–4, 130–6
psychiatry-prison continuum, 132–3,
134–5
psychologist, 77
psychology, 4; of criminal conduct,
49
psy professions, 4, 11, 17, 49
Public Accounts Committee (Canada), 43
Public Service Alliance of Canada, 28
punishment, 15, 27, 29–32, 36, 73, 96,
124, 143–4, 150, 152; alternatives
to, 31; demand for, 38; as goal, 32,
124, 143; rationale, 29, 46, 88

Quebec, 41

race, 9–10, 16, 22, 27, 34, 41, 43, 125,
152. See also Aboriginal

recidivism: criticisms of, 48–52;
defining, 52; indicators of, 52; predicting, 52, 88; problems of, 33;
rates, 5–6, 50–1; rates, as penal
management tool, 146; sanctioned, 51; scales, 48–52
record (criminal, prison), 65, 96, 102,
112
reflexivity, 9, 54–5
reform, prison, 3–4; community-
based, 125; extending outside
prison, 148; women-centred, 144
rehabilitation, 15, 18, 29, 50, 113, 139,
144; goals, 126; needs, 43
reintegration, 6, 10–11, 13–15, 18, 43,
63, 78, 81–2, 98, 125, 139, 151. See
also release
relations of ruling, 24, 129, 144
release (from prison), 16, 33, 105, 130,
134, 138, 143, 147; conditions, 50–1,
65; programs, 5; strategies, 29
release, challenges after, 12, 103–22,
112, 134–8, 143, 146–7; compounded by prison experiences,
102; employment, 107; financial,
106; interpersonal relationships,
115–18; largely linked to housing
difficulties, poverty, 103–4, 106;
and layers of state control, 123;
police intrusion and surveillance,
111; psychiatric, 131, 133
rescue and reform model, 36
researcher: feminist, 9, 15–16, 46,
56; and researched, relationship
between, 8–9; subjectivities of,
25
resiliency, 55–6
restraint chair, 85, 91, 94, 99
return (to prison), 7, 11, 51–2, 54, 65,
85, 98, 106, 114, 116, 119, 122, 133–

6, 141, 143; factors determining, 4,
8, 10, 12
risk assessment, 4, 7–8, 48–9, 138;
criticisms of, 50–1; gender-blind, 8;
LSI-R, 49
Rogers, Kimberly, 44–6, 149–50
Royal Commission of Inquiry into
the Criminal Justice System, 70,
111–12

Safe Streets Act (Ontario), 36
Saskatchewan, 41
school, 58–9, 61, 65, 71, 80, 106, 110,
152; return to, 64, 67, 107
security, 28, 35, 38, 129, 142, 149;
classification scheme, 43; as goal,
88; levels, 28; low, 47; maximum,
76; medium, 47; minimum, 47;
over-classification of, 43; private,
114
sex: bias, 28; discrimination based
on, 42; offender, 71, 109, 111, 143–4;
roles, 130
sexism, 24, 41
sexuality, 10, 20, 70; linchpin of gender inequality, 80, 151
shoplifting, 39, 62, 73–4, 79, 95, 114,
119, 136; program for, 111
single mother, 12, 39–40, 46, 60–1, 81,
107, 110, 115, 119, 136
Single Parents Association of Newfoundland, 110
social assistance, 34, 46, 59, 60, 62,
106; benefits, 138, 149; fraud, 45;
policies, 149; prolonged reliance
on, 146; rates, 39–40, 108; recipients, 149. See also welfare
social control (by the state), 4–6, 8,
12, 23, 31, 34, 36, 54, 57, 70, 74–8,
95, 111, 113, 123, 128, 130–9, 142,

145; agencies, localized, 4–6, 12,
130–45; disguised as community
groups, 6; factors propelling
women into crime, 23, 26; formal,
4–6, 74–8, 111, 130–9, 147; functions, 19; gendered, rationales for,
129; by home-care staff, 142; informal, 78–81; institutionalized, 25,
29, 125, 129; layering of, 54, 74–8,
136, 143, 146, 150; meaning of
term, 123–4; mechanisms, 26; models of, 19, 126, 129; networks, 5–6,
123; outside prisons, 29; by parole
services, 139; of probation, 134;
relations of, 34; sites of, 125; state
agents of, 130–9; strategies of, 4,
123, 126, 129; theories, 124, 129;
trajectories of, 4; transcarceral patterns of, 147; and transcarceration,
124–30, 147; of whereabouts and
activities, 112; of women, 4, 125,
129–39
social justice, 148, 152; problems of,
30–1. See also reforms
social safety net, 35, 151
social services, 18, 31, 35–6, 60, 62, 74,
129, 131, 136–9, 147
social welfare. See welfare
social work, 4; as social control, 124
socialist feminism, 11, 19–22, 151;
criticisms of, 22. See also Marxist
feminism
Springhill, 132
squeegee kids, 35–6
St John's, 39, 48, 70, 95, 105, 110, 130;
Status of Women Council, 61
standpoint feminism, 11, 22–4; criticisms of, 23
staying out (of prison), 8, 11–12, 18,
51, 54, 74, 82–4, 104, 110–12, 122,

130, 132, 135, 138, 140, 146–7; chances of, 5–6, 12
Stephenville, 47
success, 4–7, 18, 28–30, 49–54, 78, 82, 130, 146, 148; definitions of, 5, 7, 52; predictors of, 4
support, 64, 84; financial, 58, 66, 85, 119, 151; lack of, for women, 111; network, 6, 121, 141; peer, 4, 8, 82, 87; professional, 121; services, 94; systems (professional and family), 6, 35, 69, 75, 84, 87, 115–16, 118, 121, 141–2, 147; for women, 87, 134. *See also* family; interpersonal relationships
support services, 94; lack of, 87
surveillance, 4, 6, 136, 138, 143; through mandatory drug and/or alcohol testing, 37; electronic, 30–1, 48; global positioning, 31; by non-profit agencies, 147; police, 111–14
survival crimes, 38–9, 58, 95, 148. *See also* welfare, fraud; shoplifting; cheque forging

Task Force on Federally Sentenced Women, 3, 42–3
theory, 23–4; feminist, 11, 19; social control, 124, 129
transcarceration, 4–6, 12, 31, 124–30, 147
Transition House, 105, 109–10, 122, 134, 143
treatment, 6, 8, 16–19, 31, 43, 47, 74, 99, 124, 130, 132; centres, 18, 126, 129; cognitive behavioural, 15, 49, 145; discriminatory, 37–8; mandatory, 145; of prisoners, inhumane, 44–5; programs, 89, 144–5; requirements different for women, 38, 90–

1, 121; services, 19, 35, 48, 83, 89, 126–7, 129; of women, 149
Truro, 86, 90, 96–7

underemployment, 40, 107–8
unemployment, 106; rates, 40–1
United Nations Convention on the Elimination of All Forms of Discrimination Against Women, 46
United States, 36

victim, 36, 41, 70, 73, 109, 126
victimization, 70; of women, 150
victimology, 26
violence, 74–6, 80, 104; against women, 41, 44, 65–6; caused by anger, 74; in retaliation against abuse, 59, 71
voice, 24, 32, 54, 56, 152

Wales, 44
Waterford Hospital, 52, 70, 72, 76–7, 97–8, 102, 130–2, 134–6
welfare, 4, 12, 17, 20–1, 27, 62, 122–3, 127, 129–30, 135, 138–9, 143; benefits, 62; caseworkers, 5; cheque, 103, 108, 117–18; child, 69, 76–7, 103–4, 148–151; cops, 37; dependence on, 59; fraud (*see also* Rogers, Kimberly), 33, 35, 39, 45–6, 60, 62, 149; inadequate, 60; office, 45; program, 34; rates, 39–40; reforms, 45, 60, 65, 149; retrenchment, 59; state, 33, 35–6; system, 15, 33, 35–6, 56, 63, 65–6; trap, 65–6. *See also* social assistance
welfare-criminal justice complex, 4
Whitbourne, 93
working poor, 106–7